ALWAYS
TRUE

ALWAYS
TRUE

[God's 5 promises when life is hard]

JAMES MACDONALD

MOODY PUBLISHERS
CHICAGO

All Scripture quotations, unless otherwise indicated, are taken from *The Holy Bible, English Standard Version*. Copyright © 2000, 2001 by Crossway Bibles, a division of Good News Publishers. Used by permission. All rights reserved.

Scripture quotations marked NKJV are taken from the *New King James Version*. Copyright © 1982 by Thomas Nelson, Inc. Used by permission. All rights reserved.

Scripture quotations marked NASB are taken from the *New American Standard Bible*®, Copyright © 1960, 1962, 1963, 1968, 1971, 1972, 1973, 1975, 1977, 1995 by The Lockman Foundation. Used by permission. (www.Lockman.org).

Scripture quotations marked NIV are taken from the Holy Bible, New International Version®, NIV®. Copyright © 1973, 1978, 1984 by Biblica, Inc.™ Used by permission of Zondervan. All rights reserved worldwide.

Scripture quotations marked KJV are taken from the King James Version.

Published in association with the literary agency of Wolgemuth & Associates, Inc.

Cover Design: David Riley Associates

Cover Image: Maurice van der Velden/iStockphoto

Interior Design: Smartt Guys design

Library of Congress Cataloging-in-Publication Data

MacDonald, James, 1960-
Always true : God's 5 promises for when life is hard / James MacDonald.
    p. cm.
Includes bibliographical references (p.   ) and index.
ISBN 978-0-8024-5869-8
1. God (Christianity)--Promises. 2. Consolation. I. Title.
BT180.P7M33 2010
248.8'6--dc22

2010034804

We hope you enjoy this book from Moody Publishers. Our goal is to provide high-quality, thought-provoking books and products that connect truth to your real needs and challenges. For more information on other books and products written and produced from a biblical perspective, go to www.moodypublishers.com or write to:

Moody Publishers
820 N. LaSalle Boulevard
Chicago, IL 60610

1 3 5 7 9 10 8 6 4 2

Printed in the United States of America

To my dad
Verne MacDonald
Who through life's deepest valley has proven the promises of God and through his faith adorned the gospel before all who know him.

CONTENTS

Foreword

I have been loving the same man, the author of this book for more than thirty years. I have seen him face and conquer pressures and problems that could and did crush other men. I am an unashamed "fan" of my own husband. Because I see him up close and I know how deeply he strives to be a man of integrity and practice behind the scenes what he preaches to our church (and to the listeners of Walk in the Word). What he writes is also an extension of what he says and how he lives.

Having said that, I confess to a certain fear rising in my heart as the waves of adversity crashed relentlessly on the shore of our home; and for the first time ever, really knocked him down. Never in all our years have I seen my husband struggle like this; asking the hardest questions, wrestling with the deepest issues, deciding for himself if what he has preached for so long would be true for him and hold him up when life was hardest.

Yes, we talked and prayed together, but it was *his* cancer, *his* church crisis, and *his* burden as leader of our home. For months I watched him battle and search for something solid upon which he could place his weight and rise from the swamp of pain and perplexity into which I had helplessly seen him sink. I prayed fervently that our heavenly Father would fill his soul with something fresh. This book is the record of what he found. The content has fed our church and I pray that it fuels your heart too, in whatever you are facing. But before it was any of that for others, it was the rock upon which James stood.

If you are searching just now for some stability in the midst of a raging storm, you are not going to read theory or ivory tower pie-in-the-sky non-sense here. You are about to trace the path of a weary, heavy-hearted follower and find what he found to sustain him on his journey.

James is so different today because of what he has written in *Always True*. Trace his steps and you will discover afresh as he did the awesome things our great God has given to us in His promises. They truly are exceedingly great and precious. Take the time, do the work, read the whole book, because if you do—if you do, your life will be changed forever as ours has been.

Kathy MacDonald
October 2010

*As His divine power has given to us all things that pertain to life
and godliness, through the knowledge of Him who called us by glory and
virtue, **by which have been given to us exceedingly great and
precious promises** . . . 2 Peter 1:3–4 (*NKJV*)*

*What is a promise?
A promise is the assurance God gives His people so that they can
walk by faith while they wait for Him to work.*

"You can be sure"

Some reality hits like a hurricane. You board up the windows and hunker down trying to survive. You're not working out or thinking about nutrition. You're not trying to strengthen relationships. You're not thinking about your investments or your next career moves. You are just hoping the plywood you hastily hammered up holds the windows.

You just want to be alive and see the sun shine again, inside and out.

Times like these come suddenly. You were going along, doing all right, managing the ups and downs of your routine when out of nowhere, (to change the analogy) a boulder dropped from the sky and crash-landed on your life. Hardly breathing under this sudden, crushing weight, you were desperate for help to come or you weren't going to make it.

That's the place in my life where the message of this book was born.

My wife and I were confined to a living crucible of questions and events for more than two years. We didn't see it coming, and once we were in the furnace our regular resources for relief became totally inadequate. At times we didn't know if we would make it out. Some weeks I felt unable to stand up before our church family and preach another message. I didn't know if my ministry would end, and some days, I didn't care. We just wanted to survive.

Later I learned the lessons that became the book *When Life Is Hard.* But when life was hardest, I didn't need lessons—I needed life support! *What* do you preach at a time like that? You can be sure I didn't pull out some topical truths for trivial Christianity. No, leaning hard on the Lord, I delivered a series of messages called "Always True: Five Exceedingly Great and Precious Promises." Not five little pep talks to bring a momentary word of hope. No, instead we tested five major categories of promise in God's Word. Five promises God makes over and over to every person of faith in every generation. I was the man gasping and going under for the third time and these promises were my lifeline. By them I was pulled to safety—and you can be too.

Think of these five promises as an all-access backstage pass to Scripture's greatest treasure. These promises have given me such incredible hope that I know they can do the same for you. They have given us such buoyancy in the stormy waters and they can keep you from going under too. When nothing else makes sense, these promises will literally be the rock you can stand on while you wait for the better days that ARE COMING.

I am assured of this because they are the promises of God Himself.

When you need them as never before you will discover these promises to be as Scripture says, **"exceedingly great and precious,"**—but only when you put your whole weight down on them. They belong in your home on a wall in a red box with a glass front that reads: "In case of emergency, remove hammer and break glass." When you make these truths your own, they'll become intensely personal, incredibly practical, and profoundly reliable. And periodically no doubt, you will have to rediscover in a deep way just how true they really are!

Always true? Really? Yes, thanks for bringing that up. Does the idea of absolute truth cause you to raise an eyebrow? Only in God's Word can you find a statement that is invariably true. No one else but God, and nothing other than His Word, delivers a nonnegotiable, unconditional "always." If you are unconvinced or unsure that the Bible is God's Word—just give it a chance. Scripture can and will resonate in your soul and rock you to the core of your being like nothing else can. Don't wait to be convinced that the Bible is God's Word, just crack it open—give it a chance to grip your heart with hope . . . and it will! No matter what you are facing today, you can be sure that these promises are true for you, right now. Take hold of them, cherish them, believe them, and wait for God to make them reality. I have taken and proven the promises of God, and you can too.

They are always true!

In Christ who "spoke and the worlds were formed,"

James MacDonald
Fall 2010
Chicago, Illinois

Let's begin . . .

I'm sitting in my office now, listening to a song I used to sob through, and I am thinking about you.

I remember with stark vividness what it was like to have *nothing* but the promises of God. When I began to search the Scriptures for promises I did so with trembling hands and a desperate heart. I had to know what was going to happen in some incredibly dark days. I knew I could grope my way to the light if I just knew God had some hope for me that would carry me right through to the end. That's what the promises of God are all about, and I long for you to find them in a way that is quicker and easier than what I had to go through. Think for a moment . . . *God has made some promises . . .*

The very idea that God commits Himself to do anything is incredible. He doesn't have to bind Himself to us in any way. He's God—completely above and beyond us. As part of His creation, we are in no position to hold Him to anything; He owes us nothing. Before we get into our study, we must pause and get our minds around this inconceivable assertion: God flat out promises to do some things—for us. In fact, given certain circumstances, God has already told us what He will do! *That's amazing.* Second Peter 1:4 says, **"By which have been given to us exceedingly great and precious promises"** (NKJV). God has recorded some assurances and He thinks they're **"exceedingly great and precious."** I love that! Let's unpack that a bit . . .

I Promise!

It's impossible to trick our kids anymore on April Fools' Day. After years of practical jokes and all kinds of fun chicanery that Kathy and I have poured out on them, they're now wise to it all. We even have to keep our eyes peeled for counterattacks!

One year we rushed into their bedrooms at six a.m. shouting, "Get up! We're late for school!" We had changed every clock in the house to read an hour later. Our yawning offspring ran downstairs, half-dressed. We stuffed them in the car and hurried across town—only to find the school parking lot empty. Kathy and I yelled, "April Fools!" and took them out for breakfast. The days of tricking our children on April 1st are over. They see it coming for weeks ahead of time.

However, one of the fallouts from teasing them is that when I wanted to be serious about something, they hesitated to believe me, wondering if we might be playing another joke. We had to make an unbreakable rule that if I said, "I promise," they could totally, completely trust me.

Though I could not perfectly fulfill the intent of those words in every instance they know to this day that when Dad says, "I promise," he is incredibly serious and will devote himself 100 percent to what he has said.

The problem of course is that we're human. We disappoint one another all the time—even the ones we love, even when we don't mean to. Our best intentions don't always happen.

And that's where we're so much different from God. When God says, "I promise," He delivers, because He can, and nothing will thwart or delay His intention to do exactly as He has promised. He doesn't forget or get distracted . . . He cannot lie and He cannot fail. God always follows through, on time, every time! When He makes a commitment, He keeps it. When He gives His word; it's a done deal.

A promise and the Promiser

A general definition of a promise is "a declaration of what someone will do." A promise usually implies a positive, dependable consequence. If there's a promise, we believe something good is going to happen. If something bad is in the wind, we call it a threat. While God does make threats regarding the outcomes for bad behavior, those are not promises—they're a topic for a different kind of book.

What God understands and we must too, is that the character of the Promiser is on the line in every promise. Our church's longtime elder board chairman taught me that God honors the one **"who swears to his own hurt"** (Psalm 15:4). Whenever our backs were against the wall, and especially when our church was small and every decision was so critical, he insisted that our first action would always be to keep our word and do what we had promised even if the consequences were negative for us.

If we give our word, we've got to follow through. And the way the Lord values His relationship with us can't be appreciated until we realize how incredibly invested our God is in keeping His promises to us. How can we not be overwhelmed by the significance of Romans 8:32, **"He who did not spare his own Son but gave him up for us all, how will he not also with him graciously give us all things?"** Having given so much, God will surely never stop and refuse to complete in smaller things what He began to do for us in Christ.

Hang on to God's promises

How we relate to God is largely determined by what we do with His promises. All that stands between you and what He has promised you is time. This book is about learning to live with today in the reality of what God has promised is our future. Even when it's hard to trust, God's promises remain the same. Nothing can change God's stated intent. Keep in mind that God even sympathizes with the challenge it is for us to lean on His promises: **"He knows our frame; he remembers that we are dust"** (Psalm 103:14). God has not left you wondering about what's going to happen, or uncertain about the future, or overcome by fear. He makes promises to you so you can get through the long nights and the difficult days of *waiting*.

He asks you to hang on to His assurances of determined outcomes to get through the dark times when life is hard.

In the meantime . . .

The hardest moment of hanging on, of course, is the gap between believing His promise and receiving the fulfillment of that promise. The Christian life would be easy if the time was short between when you first *appeal to* God's promises and when you *receive* what He promised. If you could invoke God's pledge one day and cash it in the next, Wow—wouldn't that be great!? Forget about fast-food promises—that's not the way God works.

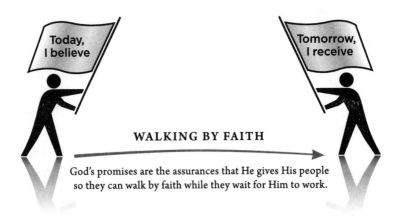

Today, I believe

Tomorrow, I receive

WALKING BY FAITH

God's promises are the assurances that He gives His people
so they can walk by faith while they wait for Him to work.

Today I believe; tomorrow (or at some point in the future) I receive. The distance between today and tomorrow is called walking by faith. The hard part is in the waiting between the promise and the answer; and even harder, when the waiting comes with more hardship or even setbacks.

Where's this going? Where am I going to end up? What does my future look like? Things aren't getting better—they're getting worse!

The reality is, we just don't know how things will play out and it's the "not knowing" that crushes us. We doubt because we don't know. We worry and despair because we can't see the outcome. We falter and sometimes fail—all because we can't stand not knowing. If only we could see for certain how this trial was going to end, we would be okay. But we don't—or we can't. So we agonize over the waiting.

I can take a bad day. I can put up with a hard month. I can even endure a lousy year or a horrendous decade if I have to, as long as I know how it will end up. But a few minutes of sheer unknowing can take me right to the edge. You may be facing a health crisis today. Or you have a burden involving your marriage or an uncertainty with a child. For someone else, it's a restlessness in your soul. Questions fill your mind. *What's up ahead? What's gonna happen to me and those I love? How will I ever get through this? Am I gonna lose it? Will I be able to endure? Will we ever be okay again?*

Our first response—waiting

Here I stand today, gripping tightly with both hands God's promises while I wait for Him to work. I couldn't go forward another day if I didn't believe what He told me. I'm anchored to one thought: God says so. For now, that's going to have to be enough.

> *God feels compassion for the pain of not knowing, and that is why He invented this idea of promise.*

Whether you realize it or not, we're in the same place. So here's what we must do: We must review His promises all the time. We must remind ourselves that our faith is in God who has never failed to do what He says. He knows what He has promised, He can't lie, and He can't forget. He will deliver on time, all the time. Who else makes promises like that? The promises are great, the outcomes are certain; all that remains is to wait on God's timing.

Again, today my faith is resting entirely on what God has said He will do.

God feels compassion for the pain of not knowing, and that is why He invented this idea of promise. It's as if He is saying, *I'm not going to leave you clueless. I'm not going to leave you wondering what I'm going to do. I don't want you to be overcome by fear. So I'm going to make you some promises to hold on to through the difficult days. You don't have to take your view of life from what you can see. You don't have to rest your happiness on what's happening right in front of you. You're not imprisoned by the crazy talk someone is putting into your head that you know isn't true. Hang on to the things I told you. What you saw clearly in the light hasn't changed just because the valley is dark.* While we wait, God gives us His promises to hold on to.

God's promises are great

Let's look at 2 Peter 1:4 again: **"By which have been given to us exceedingly great and precious promises"** (NKJV). Why are they great?

1. God's promises are great because . . . they come from a great God. The promises are huge because of who said them. Would you believe your four-year-old if he said in his best grown-up voice, "I *promise* I'll make enough money to put food on the table next month"? A promise's veracity is tied to the one who is making the commitment—and to their ability to fulfill it.

Psalm 145:3 says, **"Great is the Lord . . . ; his greatness is unsearchable."** We might as well admit it: We don't have a clue how great God is because no one can discover the depth of His greatness. Only in His promises are we able to explore and experience just how great He really is.

I love Jeremiah 32:27: **"I am the Lord. . . . Is anything too hard for Me?"** Sometimes in life, we look at our need or the overwhelming circumstances and we feel beaten before we start. But God asks, *What exactly is it that you think I can't handle?* To which we would have to reply, *Nothing is too hard for You, Lord.* Does that give you courage and hope? It does me. Holding on to God's promises is the closest we get to actually holding on to God.

2. God's promises are great because . . . they address the great issues. Don't search the Bible for silly divine assertions about surface things. God doesn't do that. The promises He makes are about big things: fear, unknowns that would paralyze us regarding our future, our family, and our finances. If your god can't promise you anything bigger than an occasional good parking place or the last piece of pizza in the box, all I can tell you is that your god is way too small!

God's pledges respond to our deepest doubts: *Am I going make it? What's going to happen up ahead? Where will those I love end up?* God makes promises about this kind of uncertainty so we won't have to wonder and worry.

God's promises are the antidote for despair. Despair is about as bad as it gets. Hope is lost: *I don't care. Nothing's going to change. It's always going to be like this. Nothing really matters anymore.* I'm sure somebody reading this is near the edge of despair. I've certainly been close to it myself in times past.

This is the time to learn from those who have navigated those dark choppy waters successfully.

David said, **"I would have despaired if I had not believed that I would see the goodness of the Lord in the land of the living"** (Psalm 27:13 NASB). *I'm not going to have to wait until heaven someday—I'm going to see God's goodness right here on this earth with my own eyes.* David said, "I would have despaired if I didn't believe that." That's the kind of stuff God's promises are about.

God's promises are great because they come from a great God and they're about great issues.

God's promises are exceedingly great

God's promises are not just great; they're *exceedingly* great—greater than anything else:

- *God's promises are greater than human wisdom.* People will fill your ears with all sorts of blah-blah-blah. Proverbs 18:2 says, **"A fool takes no pleasure in understanding, but only in expressing his opinion."** But hear this: God has spoken and He's made some promises that exceed by far the foolishness in what people often say when we are hurting.
- *God's promises are greater than white-knuckled obedience.* Have you ever been hit with a problem so big that all you can think to do is just hang on? *I'm going to get through it. Just flip a couple of pages on the calendar and wait this one out.* Rather than make you endure your trial like an endless marathon, God's promises offer strength and peace. Don't just get through your trial, get on top of it with the promises of God.
- *God's promises are greater than wallowing in self-pity.* Many people get hit by a wave of difficulty, followed by a tsunami that washes over them like a flood. Fine—have a day of that, but then rise to the surface, take hold of the promises of God, and ride the surf to shore. God will honor your faith. He's not going to let you drown.

God's exceedingly great and precious promises are your best possession:
- There's nothing remotely like them.
- They will lead you through the darkest night.

- They will carry you through the longest day.
- They will accompany you through the deepest valley.

God's promises are precious

Scripture says that His promises are **"exceedingly great and *precious*"** (NKJV, emphasis added). "Precious" is not a kindergarten word. You'll never hear a five-year-old use it. When you're young, you don't know what is valuable. You think *quick* or *cool* or *easy* is a high commodity. But the older you get, the more you realize that *precious* is best. *Precious* comes with a weight that conveys value.

The apostle Peter is infamous for his impulsive behavior. In the Gospels, he was fast, foolish, and fluctuating, more heat than light in those early days. When we meet him again thirty-five years later in 2 Peter, he has grown slower, softer, and quieter. His writing exudes time-worn wisdom. By then he knew what was precious. Just a couple of weeks after Peter wrote this final letter, he gave up his life for Jesus Christ. Church history records very reliably that Peter didn't feel worthy to be killed in the same way that Jesus was. So his executioners granted him a last request and crucified him upside down.

Peter learned a lot about what is of greatest value in this world and in our faith. He wrote of the "precious blood of Christ" (1 Peter 1:19) and described our faith as precious (1 Peter 1:7). He called believers precious stones (1 Peter 2:4). He referred to Jesus as a precious cornerstone (1 Peter 2:6) and tells us about God's precious promises (2 Peter 1:4).

"Precious" is a treasure for those who aren't in a hurry. It takes time and attentiveness to get to the place where you realize what is truly precious.

Precious also takes proving. Something isn't precious to you until you've proven it so. I've got to admit that when I hear the word "precious," I sometimes think of Gollum in the Lord of the Rings series who always croaked out, "My precious." Even in that fantasy epic, that creepy little creature believed that the ring had power and could positively alter the course of his life. It follows that something is precious to you when you understand that it can do for you what nothing else can.

When Peter defined God's promises as precious, he based his description on personal experience. He had found firsthand that hanging on to what God has said is the best way forward.

Memorizing promises

When Kathy and I were in college, we memorized a lot of Scripture, including a few wonderful biblical promises. I'm glad to have them committed to my mind, but honestly, they didn't become precious to me until years later when I had to put my full weight down on them. When God's promises hold you up and strengthen and sustain you, they become precious. They're treasured because of time. They're precious because they're proven. I have tasted and seen that the Lord is good (Psalm 34:8). I don't just know it in my head; I've experienced it in my life. He's held me up. I've seen God's faithfulness. His promises do for us what nothing else can do. They untie knots that nothing else can unravel. They allow us to climb over life's obstacles with a *God says so* confidence.

So let's go after them.

If you and I have met in God's Word before, you know that my usual way to study the Scriptures is book-by-book, chapter-by-chapter, and verse-by-verse. But this is a topical study. In order to find the great and precious promises of God's Word—and believe me, there are awesome promises to be found—you've got to be ready to turn some Bible pages. These promises are like diamonds hidden in a mountain of gold. All of Scripture is gold, but in the midst of it are these precious gems, these promises.

I would challenge you to have your Bible open as you read. Find the verses we reference for yourself and underline them in your Bible. Our fingers are going to get a bit tired, but we won't care—we're mining the greatest treasure of the universe.

When we're done, you can also visit the Scripture index in the back of this book for a list of the Scriptures we've covered in each section. Spend the time to turn to them in your Bible and review them for the treasure that they are. Have them marked and ready for review in a time of emergency. And, right from the start, make these promises your own. As soon as you realize one applies to a situation in your life, claim it, rest in it, and begin to wait attentively for God to keep His Word.

Three extra helps to make this study your own:

Theology of a promise

One of my favorite parts of this study is the section before each of the five promise chapters. There we will focus on one truth about how this whole promise thing works. "Theology of a Promise" will give a fresh definition to resting your life on the promises of God. What you believe about God is the most important thing about you. And so before we dig into each promise we will take a fresh look at the Promiser and why He has chosen to relate to us with promises.

My greatest desire for you is that as you read this book, your confidence and faith in the Lord God will grow stronger and deeper. I'm praying now that you'll love Him more passionately as a result of what you discover about His character; you'll trust Him more readily as your faith is stirred by His faithfulness to what He has promised; and you'll desire Him more unashamedly as you begin to experience the power of standing on His promises.

This can all happen with your increased understanding and faith in God Himself. We are not just seeking the gifts of His hand, but our highest goal is to increasingly know, love, and trust the Giver, the God who wrote these promises down for us.

Take to heart

At the end of every chapter you can take our definition of a promise, pull it out of the book, and put it to work in your life. I encourage you to engage with the questions. Ponder them for your own life. Can I ask you to share your thoughts with at least one person? This step can make all the difference in how this study of God's Word will impact your life. Call a friend and discuss *Always True* together. Your conversations about what you are reading and how it applies to your life may be the most important thing that happens to you through this book.

God's promises are an assurance God gives His people so they can walk by faith while they wait for Him to work.

Know by heart

Before we're done, I want you to know by heart all five of God's exceeding great and precious promises. You may already have some of these verses committed to memory. If you do, you know this investment pays huge dividends. Just take a verse at a time. Write it out on a 3 x 5 card or a sticky note and read it over, out loud, five or six times a day. Once you have it down, review it a couple of times a week and it's yours! I guarantee you won't be sorry if you take this challenge with an enthusiastic, "I'll do it!"

I believe everything that Scripture says about itself, and I want you to experience and share that confidence too. Scripture describes itself as milk (1 Peter 2:2), solid food (Hebrews 5:12–14), light (Psalm 119:105), and nourishment to your soul. By it you are warned of what could injure you and that in its study there is great reward (Psalm 19:11). Long after you forget the specifics of what you read in this book, my prayer is that you will still remember that *God's Word is real*. It's from God Himself. It's life changing. To neglect it is to starve, but to dig into it is to feed yourself and cause your soul to flourish. **"Faith comes by hearing and hearing by the Word of God"** (Romans 10:17 NJKV). The more you believe that God's Word holds life and truth, the more your faith in God will grow.

God's Word is always true—believe it.

A prayer for our journey into His promises

Thank You in advance, Lord, for what You will impress on our hearts about Yourself and Your promises in these pages. We commit ourselves afresh to believe Your Word and to listen for Your Spirit's prompting. Our lives cannot be the same once Your presence and Your promises are at home with us. Apart from You, we can do nothing.

Abide in us, Lord.
In the power of Jesus' Name, Amen.

[THEOLOGY OF A PROMISE]

God is a Promiser by nature.

GOD IS A PROMISER BY NATURE.

An important truth about God you need to treasure in your heart is that He is a Promiser and it's His nature to fulfill His promises. You can't read Scripture very long without seeing that truth revealed throughout history. He promised:

- that one of Eve's offspring would crush the serpent (Genesis 3).
- Noah that He would never again destroy the world by a flood (Genesis 9).
- innumerable descendants to Abram (Genesis 12).
- to deliver the people of Israel from slavery in Egypt (Exodus 6).
- blessings to the people of Israel for keeping the law and curses for disobeying the law (Deuteronomy 28).
- victory to Joshua over the Canaanites (Joshua 1).
- an everlasting throne to David's descendants (2 Samuel 7).

And that's just a sample. The Bible is overflowing with the promises that God has made. In the Old Testament, the Messiah is promised; in the New Testament, He arrives—and then promises to come again! God's entire communication with us can be summed up as "I promise."

The persistence of God's pledge is also true for you personally. Remember the two flags? God gives us promises so we can walk by faith between the "Today, I Believe" and "Tomorrow, I Receive" flags. Hebrews 6:17–18 gives us proof of God's goal in making promises to us: so we will be strongly encouraged to hold on.

"So when God desired to show more convincingly to the heirs of

the promise the unchangeable character of his purpose, he guaranteed it with an oath, so that by two unchangeable things, in which it is impossible for God to lie, we who have fled for refuge might have strong encouragement to hold fast to the hope set before us."

Look for evidence of God's character in those verses.

I'm floored by the fact that God promises anything. What's more, He's committed to help you see His promises because He knows what strength they will give you. He puts His weight behind wanting **"to show more convincingly."** He wants to impress upon you **"the unchangeable character of his purpose."** He wants you to be confident and solid in what you believe about Him. God doesn't want you wavering or waffling through life, or doubting or faltering in your faith. He is saying, *Take hold of life with conviction. I want you to have full assurance right to the end! Don't give up or back up or shut up. Don't quit! Go all the way with Me, all right?*

God wants you to be so familiar with His character and live so confidently in your faith that you can say, "I know what God's going to do. I don't know when or how, but He's made me some promises and I can walk by faith until I see it."

Hebrews 6:11 shows us the long view of the power of God's promises: **"And we desire each one of you to show the same earnestness to have the full assurance of hope until the end."** God doesn't want one person to quit. He doesn't desire to lose any one of us. He wants us to make our calling sure and to work out our salvation with fear and trembling (see Philippians 2:12). God puts promises in our hands so we can give a full demonstration of the reality of our conversion to Christ. Hebrews 6:12 goes on to say, **"So that you may not be sluggish, but imitators of those who through faith and patience inherit the promises."** God gives us promises we can lean on for the long haul.

Are you trusting the Lord with all your heart? Then He wants you to **"have strong encouragement to hold fast to the hope set before us"** (Hebrews 6:18b). I just love that about God. He tells us that as His children, we are called **"the heirs of the promise,"** or as I would say, "You're one of God's kids, a kid of promise." Your whole identity is tied up in the promises that He's made to you.

Isn't it time to live that way?

The Christian life includes walking by faith from the first day of your greatest problem to the final day when He reveals His most amazing solution.

The exceedingly great and precious promises that we're ready now to embrace are given to us by God, the great Promiser.

*You can put your whole weight on the promises
of God and He will hold you up.*

He will sustain you in seasons of trial.

He will walk with you in daily paths.

*He says, "I'm God and I stake My reputation on the promise
that 'I will never leave you nor forsake you.'"*

*The promise that God will always be with you
is no less than incredible.*

Promise #1: GOD IS ALWAYS WITH ME

(I will not fear)

It is the LORD who goes before you.
He will be with you; he will not leave you or forsake you.
Do not fear or be dismayed. Deuteronomy 31:8

Before we can fully rejoice in a cure for a disease, we must feel the pain and recognize the outcome of that ailment if no cure is applied. Likewise, before we can fully embrace the delight of God's promises, we must first suffer the desperateness of our need. We can only grasp how exceedingly great and precious God's promises are when we realize how much we need them.

The Bible recognizes that one of our greatest problems is fear. You can disguise fear with all kinds of costumes, or drive it undercover. But it is never very far away for any of us. Some folks are afraid of their shadow, and some recognize that their fears *are* their shadow.

The Many Faces of Fear

For just a moment, let's talk about what we fear. One word says it all; we fear the *future*. No one's afraid of the past. The past creates other problems—like regrets and consequences. And no one is exactly afraid of the present. We might be upset about the present, but we don't fear it because we know it. We fear *now* what will happen *next*. "Something's up ahead and

I don't want it." Fear is about as accurate and reliable as the local weather forecast, but both seem to specialize in creating a frenzy among people.

Loss, pain, and lots more!

When we think about the future, we fear loss and pain. We're afraid of losing people. *Will my husband always love me? Will this treasured friendship last? Will my kids walk with the Lord or go their own way?*

We're afraid of losing possessions. *I'm barely able to make ends meet; will I be able to keep my house? Will I have enough? Will there be money for my kids to go to college?*

We're afraid of losing our position. *I've worked hard; I have an opportunity. Will I always have it, or will I lose it? I'm in over my head; will they find out?*

We fear physical pain; the doctor's pokes and prods; the suffering of chronic pain due to illness that doesn't heal.

Even more, we fear emotional pain. *My friend has found another, my kids just don't care, my spouse is drifting away.*

We fear personal pain. *I'm not happy with myself. I could have, I should have, I would have, I didn't, I'm not. I failed.* Fear is always about something up ahead that I dread.

If you want some lively bedtime reading, look up *fear* on the Internet. You will find thousands of documented phobias, the ancient term we use to classify what keeps people from facing specific situations. A quick search gives us these:

Acrophobia—the fear of heights

Agoraphobia—the fear of open or public places

Anthropophobia—the fear of people

Aquaphobia—the fear of water

Astraphobia—the fear of thunder and lightning

Apparently, take any Greek word, add *phobia* to it and you've named a new fear! And that's just in the A's; let's take a quick survey of the rest of the alphabet:

Bathmophobia—the fear of stairs or steep slopes

Claustrophobia—the fear of closed spaces

Nictophobia—the fear of darkness

Numerophobia—the fear of numbers

Pyrophobia—the fear of fire

Zoophobia—the fear of animals

I'm getting bored—are you? People are afraid of a lot of stuff and it's funny until we get to the one that causes churning in our stomachs.

Let's agree that fear is a universal problem. It hits us like a wave, threatening to swallow us in its undertow. Scripture identifies the overwhelming emotion of fear almost a thousand times. The word *fear* is used 441 times; *afraid*, 167 times; *tremble*, 101 times; and *terror* or *terrified*, 121 times. The words *dread*, *frighten*, and *faint* are also repeatedly used throughout Scripture.

Let's take a look at some of these Scripture passages:

- Abraham was fearful about his lack of a male heir. God told him in Genesis 15:1, **"Fear not. . . . I am your shield; your reward shall be very great."**

- Hagar was afraid she would have to watch Ishmael die. God told her in Genesis 21:17, **"What troubles you, Hagar? Fear not, for God has heard the voice of the boy where he is."**

- The Israelites were terrified as the murderous Egyptians bore down on them from behind as they faced the barrier of the Red Sea. There was no way out. Right in the middle of that seemingly hopeless situation, Moses said to them, **"Fear not, stand firm, and see the salvation of the Lord, which he will work for you today"** (Exodus 14:13).

- David was afraid for his life on many occasions, but he penned these words in Psalm 23:4: **"Even though I walk through the valley of the shadow of death, I will fear no evil, for you are with me."**

- Solomon seriously doubted his ability to follow in his dad's footsteps in leading the nation, but David told him, **"Be strong and courageous and do it. Do not be afraid and do not be dismayed, for the Lord God, even my God, is with you. He will not leave you or forsake**

you, until all the work for the service of the house of the LORD is finished" (1 Chronicles 28:20).

- Jeremiah was afraid to tell people something they didn't want to hear. God said to him in Jeremiah 1:8, **"Do not be afraid of them, for I am with you to deliver you."**

Many of the Bible people we regard as heroes shared the same fears that are so familiar to us.

Fear is a universal problem

We can all relate to fear in one form or another. It's a primal emotion, instinctive to our human nature just like grief or anger. You don't ever say to yourself, "Well, I think I need to get afraid." You don't have to plan it; it just happens to you.

Of course the problem isn't when fear stops by for a visit. The problem is when you open the front door and invite it in. *Fear! Welcome back! I've been waiting for you. Your room is ready down the hall! No, I insist—take the master bedroom! Mi casa es su casa!* When you receive fear into your mind, heart, and life and nourish it like a friend, that's a problem. While you can't keep fear from visiting, you can slam the door in its face. With God's promise in your hand, that's exactly what you are able to do.

Fear among emotions

Some emotional responses have their place. Take anger. You could be angry about injustice or unrighteousness. That kind of righteous anger is a good thing. It drives positive action. This is exactly the kind of anger that filled Jesus as He strode through the temple courts, overturning the counters of the moneychangers and cleaning up His Father's house (see Matthew 21:12–13).

Grief is also acceptable for a season. When a loved one dies or you go through any profound loss, you need time to work through it. There is a healthy and necessary adjustment to the sudden absence of someone or something important. But grief can stay too long and eventually needs to be kicked out. Still, grief has a purpose; fear never does. Even doubt has a place. It's not wrong or harmful to doubt sometimes. You can doubt a decision or an opinion. You can doubt a path you've gone down. It's not always wrong to doubt, but it's always wrong to fear.

Some sins grab and imprison you. Fear will do that. Dread chains you in a small, dark room and sinks its clammy claws into your spirit. Terror is tough to shake. Once you've given it a place in your heart, it becomes an addictive drug you can't live without.

Why fear is not okay

Fear expresses the opposite of all that Christianity is to be. Fear is the contradiction of faith. Faith says, "Whatever it is, it'll be okay because of God." Fear says, *It's not going to be okay*, and doesn't think much about God at all.

Fear is the complete state of anti-God. God seldom seems further from you than when your heart is filled with fear. Fear is relying completely on your own resources and realizing suddenly that they aren't nearly enough to sustain you. Fear has no place in the life of a Christian. A fearful response, as in an anxious, frightened reaction, is never good and never from God. Romans 8:15 tells us, **"You did not receive the spirit of slavery to fall back into fear,"** and 2 Timothy 1:7 says, **"God gave us a spirit not of fear but of power and love and self-control."**

I think you get it. Fear doesn't belong in your life.

Out with fear and in with faith.

First Promise: God is Always with Me.

The antidote for fear is the promise of God's presence. *God is with you.* "For He has said, '**I will never leave you nor forsake you.**' So we can confidently say, '**The Lord is my helper;** *I will not fear*; **what can man do to me?**'" (Hebrews 13:5–6, emphasis added). *God is with me wherever I go. How could I be afraid?*

Let the calm, strong assurance of our first great and precious promise settle down in your soul: *God is always with me. Therefore, I will not fear.*

Always in His presence

Now "God is always with me" includes more than the fact of God's omnipresence. Yes, God is everywhere; therefore He is where we are. In the truest sense, God is not in *our* presence, we are in *His* presence. Distance makes no difference to God.

David said in Psalm 139:7–10, **"Where shall I go from your Spirit? Or where shall I flee from your presence? If I ascend to heaven, you are there! If I make my bed in Sheol, you are there! If I take the wings of the morning and dwell in the uttermost parts of the sea, even there your hand shall lead me, and your right hand shall hold me."** God *is* everywhere.

I love Jeremiah 23:23–24. **"Can a man hide himself in secret places?"** As in, *God will never find me over here!* God says, **"Do I not fill heaven and earth?"** You can't hide from God. He is everywhere.

To the believer in Jesus Christ, this first promise is that God is with us *individually*. There's a special sense in which God is with each of us personally as one of His children. He is like the closest friend sitting next to us in a stadium full of strangers. He is with us in a way that is different from what an unbeliever experiences. This is the sense in which *with* us also means *for* us, as in Romans 8:31, **"What then shall we say to these things? If God is for us, who can be against us?"**

Furthermore, when you're going through hardship, or when you're heavyhearted and burdened, God rolls up His sleeves and moves toward you in a way that's unlike any other time. It doesn't matter if you can see Him working. His approach may not cause you to feel any different. But it's the truth—God is right there with you. The harder the days get, the closer He leans in so you can hear His voice. Sometimes it feels like God backs away from you when you hit hard times, but that's not true. Psalm 34:18 says, **"The LORD is near to the brokenhearted and saves the crushed in spirit."** Is your heart breaking today? God is rushing toward you. He stands there with you in the fire. I couldn't feel it at the time, but looking back, God has been right there with me during my darkest days. He gave me the wisdom to make the choices that lead me out of a very deep valley. He gave the strength that kept me from wandering off the path into deepest despair. He prompted the friend to call at just the right moment. He caused the sun to peek through. I truly would not have survived the last few years without God's abiding presence in my life. One of the places God met me most was in His Word. March of 2008 was the bottom of the bottom for me— all darkness and no light. I couldn't pray—or even think of something to ask God for—the way was so dark and lonely. It truly seemed that the circumstances would never change or improve in any way. As I wept and wondered and wandered through Isaiah I was floored by the clear word in Isaiah 60:20–21, **"Your sun shall no more go down, nor your moon withdraw itself; for the LORD will be your everlasting light, and your days of mourning shall be ended. Your people shall all be righteous; they shall possess the land forever, the branch of my planting, the work of my hands, that I might be glorified."** The presence of God could not have been more obvious to me if He had appeared visibly in the room. I know those were God's affirming words to me and quickly marked the margin of my Bible.

Scripture assures us that Jesus Himself is praying for you. *This minute.* Hebrews 7:25 makes this amazing statement: **"Consequently, [Jesus] is able to save to the uttermost those who draw near to God through him, since he always lives to make intercession for them."** Jesus lives to intercede for you. Amazing! That word *intercede* includes the sense of *pleading*— Jesus is continuously and persuasively presenting you before His Father! Before you ever kneel down to pour out your heart to God, Jesus Christ has already called out to His Father on your behalf. Even before you ask, He knows from firsthand contact what you need—because He's *with* you.

I remember this quote from my college years: "If you could hear the Lord praying for you in the next room, you would not fear a thousand enemies." Right where you are this moment, think of the Lord Jesus as in the next room, on His knees in front of the couch or a chair. His nail-pierced hands are held out and He's lifting you and your need to His Father. He knows your exact situation. He's asking His Father: "Give her strength, Lord." "Give him wisdom, God." "Give them patience. They're going to wreck it on their own,

Lord. Give them faith that will overcome their fear!" It's an incredible assertion throughout Scripture that Jesus Christ is not only *with* you, He's actually interceding for you. With even more assurance, you can be certain that God listens when His Son is praying!

Hear the words Jesus prayed for you in John 17:13–19:

> **But now I am coming to you, and these things I speak in the world, that they may have my joy fulfilled in themselves. I have given them your word, and the world has hated them because they are not of the world, just as I am not of the world. I do not ask that you take them out of the world, but that you keep them from the evil one. They are not of the world, just as I am not of the world. Sanctify them in the truth; your word is truth. As you sent me into the world, so I have sent them into the world. And for their sake I consecrate myself, that they also may be sanctified in truth.**

I Will Not Fear: God Is Always With Me.

That is a great promise, James, but isn't God with everyone?

That's a good question. Scripture, as we will see, actually says *no, He's not.* Certain attitudes actually repel God's intimate presence. His omnipresence is never reduced, but His accessible presence is withheld. He's there, but as far as we're concerned He might as well not be. The real war, of course, is fought on the inside. He won't show up when these internal attitude sins push Him away.

God is not "with" the proud

What significant human problem does not begin with pride? Psalm 138:6 says, **"The LORD . . . regards the lowly, but the haughty he knows from afar."** If you think you don't need God and can do life on your own, then God respects your choice and stays far away. A proud soul thinks that God is just for weak people. And God backs away and watches. *We'll see how that goes for you.* Pride is God repellent. Psalm 2 says He even laughs at the ludicrous claim by any of us that we're not in the "weak people" category!

A couple years ago my friend Greg Laurie was on the television talk show *Larry King Live*. King was exploring the whole topic of God and suffering. He said to Greg, "Isn't the whole idea of praying to God a crutch? I mean, if I've got breast cancer, don't I have to pray to something?"

Greg had this amazing response: "Thank God for that crutch, Larry! God's not a crutch to me; He's the whole hospital!"[1]

God rushes to help the humble person.

God is not "with" the worldly

James 4:4 says, **"Do you not know that friendship with the world is enmity with God? Therefore whoever wishes to be a friend of the world makes himself an enemy of God."** Love for the world and love for God cannot coexist. We all live in this battle. The world tries to drag us down and God wants to pull us out.

What is the pattern of your life concerning these things? Do you love what the world loves—status, possessions, ambition? It's not that we don't all feel the encroachment of the world, but if your goal is fixed on satisfying your own self-indulgence and private pleasure, and in getting what you want when you want it, you're worldly. When the attitudes and ambitions that characterize the world also characterize you, you're not in a good place no matter how many Facebook friends you have.

When God sees your preoccupation with worldly things, He questions, *You think that's so great? You think that's better than Me? You think that can satisfy you and give you what I can't give you? Go for it. Have it till you're sick of it. I'll just wait over here.* God wants nothing to do with such fleshly approaches to life.

God is not "with" the rebellious

Can't you just hear God's exasperation in Isaiah 1:5 and 15? **"Why will you continue to rebel? . . . When you spread out your hands, I will hide my eyes from you."** God is clear: *You think you're in charge, but if you come to Me with that independent "I'll do it my way" spirit, I won't even look at you. I can't tolerate that heart—not with that attitude.* God tries to get a piece of information to the rebellious and they stiff-arm Him with, *My thing is still* *working. I don't need You yet. Not me. Not now. Maybe another day I'll listen.* We always think we have another day, but Psalm 95:7–8 warns us to listen today and not to harden our hearts. Trace the pattern through the Bible; God doesn't put up with rebellion. Sooner or later, He crushes it.

He *is* with you if your heart is yielded to Him.

God is not "with" those who harbor sin

Listen up, friend. This warning is very important for all of us. James 3:2 says that **"we all stumble in many ways."** None of us are perfect people—just forgiven! That said, our relationship with God is dependent on how we deal with our own sin. How seriously we take our sin defines who we become. If we repent of our sin as soon as we realize it, if we go to God in humility, asking Him for forgiveness and strength to not return to that sin again, God's mercy floods over us. But if we downplay our sin, thinking, *No one's going to stop me from doing what I want to do. I don't care that it's sin; I'm doing it anyway,* that attitude is called "harboring sin" and it has dangerous and eternal consequences. Psalm 66:18 says, **"If I regard iniquity in my heart, the Lord will not hear"** (NKJV). The first consequence of harboring sin is cutting yourself off from God. If you tolerate your sin, you're choosing to render your prayer life worthless. Pray all you want, but it's just going to hit the ceiling.

> He *is* with you if your heart is yielded to Him.

But how can I ever get out of this if God won't hear me? God will always hear a contrite, repentant heart but He will only hear you on this subject. So if you come to Him and you're harboring a secret, private sin that you won't deal with, God will say, "Oh, good, you've come to talk about this sin?" But if you're like, "No, I've actually got something else I need," God will respond with, "Sorry, the next thing *is* your sin issue. Come back when you're ready to deal with that!"

Categorically, the Lord is not with everyone—not with the proud or the worldly, not with the rebellious or the one who harbors sin—but He can be with *you*. He *is* with you if your heart is yielded to Him; if you've turned from your sin and embraced Christ by faith and you are now seeking every day to walk in obedience to Him. And if you know as a believer that sometimes pride, worldliness, rebellion, and harboring sin still harass your life from time to time, thank God for the awareness, confess those sins, and return to fellowship with Him.

> *And since God has already given you His best, won't He also hear your prayer for anything less?*

One of the greatest treasures in the universe is the promise that God will be with us. As our Defender, Helper, Sovereign Lord, and Savior, He stands beside us and says, **"I will never leave you nor forsake you"** (Hebrews 13:5). "Never leave" means that He will always be there; "nor forsake" means that He will always be working on your behalf. He's not standing around with His arms folded. God is at work on your behalf—even when you don't see it!

God is for us! Proof: **He gave His Son**

Romans 8:31 is the best news of the day. **"What then shall we say to these things? If God is for us, who can be against us?"** What problem is too big? What enemy is too strong? Who's gonna take you on with God standing beside you? God is *for* you!

Do you get what that means? The next verse amplifies, **"He who did not spare his own Son but gave him up for us all, how will he not also with him graciously give us all things?"** God gave His only Son for you. His pure, sinless, perfect Son took the punishment for your sins and for mine. There's no gift better than that.

And since God has already given you His best, won't He also hear your prayer for anything less? Having an infinite capacity to give and having already given His best, there's nothing you can ask from God that isn't incredibly and significantly less than what He's already given. That's why we come before the throne with boldness and confidence when we ask anything of Him, because **"how will he not also . . . graciously give us all things?"**

God is for us! Proof: **He defends us.**

Romans 8:33–34 says, **"Who shall bring any charge against God's elect?"** Who can accuse us? Who can tear us down before God? God is the One who justifies. He's the Judge. He drops the gavel and makes the final decision. The passage continues, **"Who is to condemn? Christ Jesus is the one who died—more than that, who was raised—who is at the right hand of God, who indeed is interceding for us."** He knows all about us—every secret insecurity, every private struggle. And rather than condemn us, Jesus Christ prays for us. Doesn't that truth alone cause your spirit to rise up in grateful confidence?

God is for us! Proof: **He helps us.**

Back to Hebrews 13:5–6: **"For He has said, 'I will never leave you nor forsake you.' So we can confidently say, 'The Lord is my helper.'"** My security is from God. My security is not in the stock market, nor in a successful career, nor in wise family decisions or in my own abilities. All those things can vanish in a moment.

It Isn't Just Words

God is with you. Isn't that just typical of what a pastor would say? I figured you might be thinking that. *God is with you, brother. And you, sister.* But what does that really mean? How exactly does that work?

During the development of this teaching, Kathy and I were going through a very difficult season. It involved one of our kids. If you're a parent, you know the pain of this crucible. Through every intense, heart-wrenching moment of this trial, God's presence became increasingly real—so real we could touch it. Kathy and I did everything we could as parents—and it wasn't enough. There was a gap of helplessness, fear, and even anger that drove home the point that we are not ultimately in control (a hard thing to face as a parent). As we came to the end of our resources, ideas, and strength, Kathy and I had to put everything on the line for the promise of God's unchanging presence: **"'I will never leave you nor forsake you.' So we can confidently say, 'The Lord is my helper; I will not fear; what can man do**

to me?'" (Hebrews 13:5–6). We discovered again this fact: you can put your whole weight on this promise and it holds you up. It sustains you.

Letting your children feel the weight of their own wrong choices is the most painful thing we have ever endured. Yes, it was the right thing to do, but it was so hard! I am convinced we would not have been able to remain firm apart from our experience of God's presence with us. Looking back now, it was the turning point in God's work, but initially things got worse rather than better. I am so thankful that God's presence kept us moving forward in faith: **"Even though I walk through the valley of the shadow of death, I will fear no evil, for you are with me; your rod and your staff, they comfort me"** (Psalm 23:4).

Yes, but you're a pastor, James. You're duty-bound to do the biblical thing. What about regular pew-sitters like me?

Why Dan said, "I still have everything."

Meet Dan. He's a faithful follower of Jesus who is part of our church. He has graciously given me permission to tell part of his story. Until a few months ago, Dan was a senior partner at Bear Stearns Companies, one of the world's largest global investment banks, securities trading, and broker-age firms. Dan worked there for twenty-five years and was very successful. The company was solid; blue chip year after year, with 18 billion dollars in capital. Dan didn't have a whole lot to worry about until . . .

Did you ever see *It's a Wonderful Life*? Remember when everyone ran to the Building and Loan to withdraw their savings because they heard that the bank was running out of money? Everyone rushed to the tellers, shouting and demanding their cash. The whole bank was about to collapse since everybody wanted all of their money the same day.

That's what happened to Bear Stearns in 2008. Over the course of the year, and then finally over a couple of days, their stock value went from $165 a share to $2 a share. People "ran the bank," and the company collapsed. One day Dan and his colleagues were solid and stable, and a couple of dizzying days later, they were bankrupt. The whirlwind of events was completely out of their control. The disaster blindsided everyone. Dan lost *everything*.

That's so sad, you might think. *How's it going for Dan?* The surprising answer is *great*. He's full of joy and praising the Lord. *Unbelievable!* As events unfolded, I was on the phone regularly with him, checking on how he was coping. Coping? Dan was filled with the presence of the Lord. He said, "James, my heart goes out to the people around me. They're collapsing at their desks in tears. They really have lost everything." (Hear this, oh skeptic!) He added, "But I still have everything. I have the Lord! **The LORD is on my side.** The Lord is my Helper. **I will not fear. What can man do to me?**" (Psalm 118:6). Dan was going around his dying company, sharing the Lord with people in their darkest, most desperate hour. He is an amazing example of what the Lord's presence can mean practically to you.

> The harder the trial, the closer He moves toward you.

Now how can you explain that? I'm telling you: The Lord is with him, and that story isn't finished yet. Dan is finding, as you can, that you can put your whole weight down on God's great and precious promise that *He will always be with you* and it will sustain you.

The promise of God's presence got Dan through the crisis and the promise of God's provision (yet to come) got Dan back on his feet again. Eventually Dan found employment and saw his financial picture stabilize and begin to grow again. Best of all, Dan recently informed me that God is using his life as never before. Dan often says he would not want to be the person he was before this disaster changed things. He knows God and he went through these hard days together, and that has made all the difference.

Commit this to your heart

I've saved this verse for last because this is the one I want you to memorize: **"Be strong and courageous. Do not fear or be in dread of them, for it is the LORD your God who goes with you. He will not leave you or forsake you"** (Deuteronomy 31:6).

It's all there in that verse, isn't it? Take a moment and savor it again.

Whoever the "them" is, they don't have a chance!

Let's get the context. Moses and the second generation of the post-Egypt children of Israel are standing on the border of the Promised Land. Moses knows he's about to die. All the parents and grandparents of Israel had camped on this very spot thirty-eight years before, but they had doubted that God was with them and would protect them when they entered the Promised Land. All of them died in the wilderness. God is now going to give to the children what the parents wouldn't trust Him for. So Moses, on the exit ramp to heaven, delivers these marching orders (which I have summarized):

"Before you go up to face those giants in the land, you might think they are too strong for you as your parents thought. But keep in mind, *God is with you.* You're going to battle some violent opposition; you might be tempted to retreat. But reconsider—*God is with you.* You'll face overwhelming odds; you'll be incredibly outnumbered. Fear would be your natural inclination. But keep in mind, *God is with you.* This fight is not going to be over in ten minutes or ten weeks; there's no quick solution. If you think it's taking too long, remember, *God is with you.*"

"Be strong and courageous," the weathered old leader added. **"Do not fear or be in dread of them, for it is the LORD your God who goes with you. He will not leave you or forsake you"** (Deuteronomy 31:6). *Haven't we learned this to be true in these forty years?* I can picture Moses saying, *He never left us while we were in the wilderness. He never forsook us, but always provided whatever we needed. Why on earth should you fear now?*

Now as then, the worse the days get, the more God is with you. The harder the trial, the closer He moves toward you. Are you feeling crushed? He is rushing toward you to stand by your side and help you.

The best of all—God is with us

I like studying the lives of famous preachers. One of my absolute favorites is John Wesley from the 1700s. Wesley started a powerful revival in the United Kingdom, bringing tens of thousands to Christ through his ministry. The frontier circuit riders in America who preached the gospel from town to town were mostly following in Wesley's hoofprints. God literally changed the world through Wesley. His life has been such an inspiration to me that we named our second son Landon Wesley.

A lot can be taken from someone's final words since, in the end, we speak from our deepest souls. We have it on good testimony that on his deathbed Wesley exclaimed, "Best of all, God is with us." Dying in those days was a group experience. People gathered to converse (and observe) people leave this life. With his last breath, Wesley repeated what had been most precious to him, "Best of all, God is with us."[22]

"Even though I walk through the valley of the shadow of death . . . you are with me" (Psalm 23:4).

The God who knows the end from the beginning has made some promises. This first one is a great one: *God is with me. God is with you. We have nothing to fear.*

Father, for all of us who daily need to renew our confidence and faith in You, help us now to lay hold of Your promise that You will never leave us nor forsake us. Help us to speak and live fearlessly because we are aware we are in Your presence.

Lord, You are with me. You are praying for me. I am not alone. Is there any greater assurance that I should not fear? Your promise stands, spoken over and over again in Your Word and satisfying Your followers throughout thousands of years—You are with me. I commit this truth to my heart right now. May the realization that this is our challenge, our trial, and our burden strengthen and sustain me today.

In the power of Your Name, Amen.

TAKE TO HEART

GOD'S PROMISES ARE AN ASSURANCE GOD GIVES HIS PEOPLE SO
THEY CAN WALK BY FAITH WHILE THEY WAIT FOR HIM TO WORK.

Ask yourself the following questions, pausing after each to consider your answer. Consider pulling out a notebook and writing your answers.

In what ways do I struggle with fear?

What is the fear?

What can God do about the thing(s) I fear?

Is that the reason I sometimes feel so far from God when I need Him most—because I don't believe He can handle what I fear?

In what ways do I play the "What if . . ." game in my mind? What if I lose my job, What if she leaves me, What if I fail . . . ?

Does fear ever factor into my decisions? I can't do that because what if "xyz" happens?

Receive this by faith. Take a moment and scan back over your life this week. Think of the places you've been. Think of what you thought about or stressed over. *Is that too hard for God?* "**The LORD your God is with you wherever you go**," God told Joshua (Joshua 1:9). With that concept taken to heart, *what do you have to fear?*

Which of the concepts covered in this promise spoke directly to my fears?

How can I now walk by faith until God's promises are realized in my life?

KNOW BY HEART
Deuteronomy 31:6

"**Be strong and courageous. Do not fear or be in dread of them, for it is the LORD your God who goes with you. He will not leave you or forsake you.**"

[THEOLOGY OF A PROMISE]

God is a Promiser by nature.

God keeps all of His promises.

THEOLOGY OF A PROMISE

GOD KEEPS HIS PROMISES.

I'm never going to think about the Christian life in the same way again after this study.

The Christian life is about God's promises and our faith in what He said He will do. In our walk with Christ, we need to keep going—keep loving, serving, obeying—until we get what God promised. We don't have all He promised yet. In fact, we don't have even the smallest fraction of it. There is so much yet to come. So press on and wait in faith, and someday He'll fulfill all He said He would do.

You and I may have the most noble of intentions but our best promise means, *I want to; I intend to; I'll try my best.* But we all know that only time will tell. It's not like that with God. When God promises, He's not saying, *I'll try.* He means, *I can and I will!*

Who else can say that? A well-intentioned homebuyer takes out a loan, but he or she may not make good on it. The bank tries to insure the loan, but as we've learned in our country, even large financial institutions can't always come through on what they've committed to do.

I'm embarrassed every time I hear through the grapevine that another preacher has been exposed as a failure and a phony. I'm saddened every time I hear in the news about the latest police scam or politician's moral collapse. People charged with the trust to serve the public make all kinds of promises, but they don't always keep them.

In our first "Theology of a Promise" we looked at Hebrews 6:17–18 and learned that God is a Promiser by nature and that His character and His

> 1 Corinthians 2:9 says, "No eye has seen, nor ear heard, nor the heart of man imagined, what God has prepared for those who love him."

Word will never change. A few verses earlier in Hebrews 6, the writer encouraged us in our walk with Christ: **"And we desire each one of you to show the same earnestness to have the full assurance of hope until the end, so that you may not be sluggish, but imitators of those who through faith and patience inherit the promises"** (vv. 11–12).

How often do you feel sluggish in your faith? Are you in a sluggish season right now? Is the spark and passion you used to have replaced by lethargy and apathy? That's not what God wants for you, says Hebrews 6:12. He wants you to be **"imitators of those who through faith and patience inherit the promises."**

Covenants and Conditions

Before we go on, we need a bit of context about those promises. The next verse, Hebrews 6:13, reads, **"For when God made a promise to Abraham, since he had no one greater by whom to swear, he swore by himself."**

The Bible contains two kinds of promises, sometimes called "covenants." A *conditional covenant* includes your part and God's part. *I do my part, then God does His part.* The Mosaic covenant in Exodus 19–24 was an example of a conditional promise. God said, *If you obey Me, you'll be blessed. If you disobey, you'll be judged.*

An *unconditional covenant* involves only God. He carries the weight of both parties. God says, *I'm going to make this promise on My character alone. You don't have to do anything.* There are no conditions we need to meet for this promise to be realized.

The Abrahamic covenant in Genesis 12 was an unconditional covenant. God chose a people for Himself while only the future father of the nation was there to witness God's promise.

A covenant is a serious commitment. The word *covenant* actually means "to make a cut." In the Old Testament, the two parties involved in the covenant had a ceremony. They took a sacrificial animal, killed it, and cut it in half the long way. Then they separated the animal on the ground, stood between the two halves, shook hands, and swore that whatever they had committed to would be done, sealing the deal.

When God made an unconditional covenant with Abraham, He went through the whole ceremony by Himself. He put Abraham to sleep and stood alone between the pieces of the sacrificial animals. He was stating that He would fulfill this commitment no matter what Abraham did. You can read Genesis 15 to see how this jaw-dropping event went down.

Genesis 15:17 picks up at the end of the ceremony: **"When the sun had gone down and it was dark, behold, a smoking fire pot and a flaming torch passed between these pieces. On that day the LORD made a covenant with Abram, saying, 'To your offspring I give this land.'"**

Regardless of what Abraham would do, God said, "I will give you the land, and I will bless you, and multiply you."

Back to Hebrews 6. (I told you that we would be traveling all through the Bible in this study. Isn't it great to see God's hand at work throughout His Word?) God's unconditional promise is what is being talked about here. When it came time to seal the deal, God didn't have anyone greater than himself to swear by, so Hebrews 6:13 says He swore by His own character! Then He said, **"Surely I will bless you and multiply you"** (v.14). Abraham hung on to the promise, walking patiently in faith, and verse 15 says he received it: **"And thus Abraham, having patiently waited, obtained the promise."** This example is used again in greater detail in Hebrews 11:8–19.

God does not forget

Let's look once more at Hebrews 6:17: **"So when God desired to show more convincingly to the heirs of the promise the unchangeable character of his purpose, he guaranteed it with an oath."** These *purposes*, the promises that God has made, cannot change. He guaranteed them with two unchangeable things: His character and His Word.

It's outside our human makeup for us to even imagine "unchangeable." We've never experienced anything so secure and solid. We instinctively know that Jesus was speaking the truth when He said, **"Heaven and earth will pass away,"** but we are prone to wonder whether He really meant the second part, **"but my words will not pass away"** (Matthew 24:35). No one but God can make a claim like that—and keep it! Unchangeable words from an unchangeable God: **"Jesus Christ is the same yesterday and to-day and forever"** (Hebrews 13:8).

One of the things that Kathy and my kids tease me about is that I forget stuff. I'll rent a movie and say to Kathy, "I thought this looked good. I don't think there's any garbage in it."

And she'll say, "Yes, dear, we know that it's good because we watched it two weeks ago." So she'll go read a book and I'll put it in again to find out what happens because I honestly can't remember any of it. This is not one of my better characteristics.

Unfortunately, it comes up in relationships, too. I'll meet up with some guy and he'll mention that he golfs. Then I'll say, "I love to golf. We should go golfing."

And he'll look at me oddly and ask, "You mean like we did a month ago?"

"Right!" I don't know why, but I don't have a very good memory for certain things.

Fortunately, God is nothing like that. He forgets nothing and does not change. He's a Rock. When God says something, you can be sure He'll do it. When God fulfilled His promise to Abraham, He included you in that promise too. Galatians 3:29 says that **"if you are Christ's, then you are Abraham's offspring, heirs according to the promise."** You're in on all of this.

God cannot lie

We've already been over the next passage several times, but it's so important, let's take another run at it: **"So when God desired to show more convincingly to the heirs of the promise the unchangeable character of his purpose, he guaranteed it with an oath, so that by two unchange-**

able things, *in which it is impossible for God to lie*, we who have fled for refuge might have strong encouragement to hold fast to the hope set before us" (Hebrews 6:17–18, emphasis added).

God is truth! He invented truth, and everything about Him is truth. It's not simply *hard* for God to lie—that would be an issue of validity. It's not *unlikely* that God would lie—that would be a matter of probability. It is *impossible* for God to lie—that's an aspect of God's inviolable attributes—one of the things God *cannot* and therefore *will not* do.

Think of all of the reasons why people lie. Even if God could lie, He would have no motivation. He can gain nothing by lying. Everything He wants to have happen happens. All He says is true. He's afraid of nothing. He's right about everything. He's God!

Satan, as the ultimate antithesis of God, is a liar. John 8:44 says, "**[Satan] is a liar and the father of lies.**" He cannot tell the truth. Not one time has he even mentioned the truth to you unless it was wrapped in a deceptive lie. That was the tactic he used with Jesus when they met in the wilderness (Matthew 4:1–11). The devil quoted Scripture to Jesus but only to twist it for his manipulative purposes. Satan is the worst liar, while God is the ultimate truth teller. You can't count on anything Satan tells you; but you can rest the full weight of your life on God's Word.

God is not fickle

When I was a young youth pastor in Canada, there was this guy in our church who decided he was going on a mission project. It was a pretty ambitious plan, but we all chipped in and raised his support. Our church consisted of around 150 people, so sending someone to Africa was a huge deal.

Weeks went by as he packed his stuff in trunks and sent it on ahead. We bought him this special one-way ticket. On Send-off-Sunday we gathered around him and prayed over him and told him how much we loved and believed in him. After the service, we went down to "fellowship hall" (the basement) and had a big luncheon together. We embraced and cried and told him, "God's going to use you," and "Off you go." Someone took him to the airport in the afternoon.

Well, Sunday night service came around and we were back at church again. And guess who was there? Our missionary!

"What are you doing here?"

"Oh!" he said, "when I found out how much people love me, I just couldn't go!" And he never did. He said he was going to go. He raised money to go. We prayed over him to go. Someone took him to the airport, but he changed his mind! Crazy!

We smile at that now, but the story does remind us that we're fickle. We get fired up and say, "I'm going to do this or go here," and, "This is what matters to me." But later we say, "Forget about that; now it's this." Fickle! But God is not like that. God does not waver or change His mind. Joshua 23:14 reminds us, **"Not one word has failed of all the good things that the Lord your God promised concerning you. All have come to pass for you; not one of them has failed."**

Some of our promises are *Yes*, but some are also *We'll see*, or *I'll try hard*, and even *I really hope so*. Some of our promises become, *I forgot*. But God knows what He said. He can't lie and it will never slip His mind. He'll deliver, on time, every time.

Take a deep breath and take this to heart: God has *nothing* to do with broken promises. When He says, *I promise,* mark it down—it's going to happen. God keeps His promises.

I have never, not one time in my life, trusted God and regretted it. But I could fill pages with stories of the times when I've doubted God and made bad choices. God has never let me down! His sovereignty has always been at work. You don't have to be worried about whether you can trust Him. God will be faithful to Himself and to His promises.

Promise #2: GOD IS ALWAYS IN CONTROL
(I will not doubt)

Trust in the LORD with all your heart, and do not lean on your own understanding. In all your ways acknowledge him, and he will make straight your paths. Proverbs 3:5–6

Christians don't generally set out to doubt God. We don't call our faith into question without reason. For most of us, life's pain simply catches us off guard. We spiral fast when we're left on our own to deal with doubts and questions that trap our reason in a downward vortex.

Someone has said that doubt is cancer of the soul. Like a wrecking ball against your house, doubt pounds away and damages the structure of the most important thing about you—what you believe about God.

However, if in times of doubt we take our questions directly to the Lord, then our faith increases. We can't claim we won't doubt; instead, we aim toward knowing what to do with doubts when they do come at us. The promises of God and His character can stand under the most microscopic scrutiny. Doubts should drive us back to God's promises, not cause us to back away from Him! When you say, *I don't know exactly what God is doing, but I know He's in control*—that's evidence you're trusting Him. You don't realize how much you need God's promises until your smooth and easy life suddenly turns sideways. That is the time to dig into God's Word and get something to wrap your faith around.

Doubt is a lack of confidence or assurance that God will keep His promises.

Faith is an active confidence that God's promises are always true.

Conquer the wave of doubt

James 1:6 says we should pray with faith, or more specifically, we should pray *without doubt*. James must have remembered what it was like to sail during a time when ships were at the mercy of the winds and waves. He said, **"the one who doubts is like a wave of the sea that is driven and tossed by the wind."** Unstable. Back and forth in a constant state of disruption. Ugh—makes me seasick. Doubt does that.

As recorded in the Gospels, it was between three and four o'clock in the morning when the disciples got caught in a storm on the Sea of Galilee. Four or five of the twelve were experienced fisherman—they knew enough about the reputation of the lake to be terrified! The rest of the disciples took their cue from the experts. If a fisherman like Peter was scared, shouldn't they be? Just when the wind and the waves were taking them under, Jesus walked by—on the water! Crazy! Matthew 14:26 tells us that the disciples **"cried out in fear."** Verses 27–28 continue, **"But immediately Jesus spoke to them, saying, 'Take heart; it is I. Do not be afraid.'"**

Why do you doubt? He asked him. *I'm right here.*

And Peter said to him in Matthew 14:28. **"Lord, if it is You, command me to come to You on the water."** I love this about Peter. He's like, *If Jesus says I can walk on water, I can.* So Jesus said, **"Come"** And in response, **"Peter got out of the boat and walked on the water and came to Jesus. But when he saw the wind, he was afraid, and beginning to sink he cried out, 'Lord, save me'"** (vv. 29–30).

Aw Peter! You were doing so good—what happened?

I'll tell you what happened—he took his eyes off the Lord. Does that ever happen to you? When your eyes were on the Lord, life was good no matter what was going on around you. But the moment you got focused on the wind and waves, you started to sink.

How's that going with you today? If you're going under, I can guarantee it's because you've been looking at the waves (like the pitch and roll of your retirement funds). You've been listening to the howling wind (like the constant voices of doom and gloom that are rampant in our society). You have been taking your cues from what others are saying or the way they are acting instead of keeping your mind *stayed* on Christ (Isaiah 26:3). I've certainly been there. I know how that uncertainty looks and sounds. We can do better!

When our church construction project was several million over budget, and the work was halted due to "irregularities in the steel," bankruptcy loomed like dark clouds on the horizon, closing fast. I struggled to keep preaching, knowing that any day it could all be over. The critics were many and most of the critiques were fair—but didn't God's faithfulness extend even to my well-intentioned bad decisions? Doubts, fears, regrets, those were the waves that drew my attention away from the Lord. A few friends and God's grace through them provided the strength to keep my eyes fixed upon Christ. Years later, the church is healthy and strong. The ferociousness of the storm is a distant memory. But when the winds were howling, and I felt myself sinking, the turning point was truly the choice to look away from what caused doubt and keep my eyes on the Promise Keeper.

Live by Faith

Let's continue in verse 31: **"Jesus immediately reached out his hand and took hold of him, saying to him, 'O you of little faith, why did you doubt?'"** There's our word right there: *doubt*. Jesus pointed to the core problem. It wasn't that Peter noticed the wind and waves, or even that he feared when he realized where he was—he got in trouble when he let what he saw lead him to doubt instead of gazing on the One who could keep his faith strong!

The Christian way is a life of faith. In order to hold on to the promises of God, you've got to believe them and live by them. You've got to say to yourself, *I believe this promise is true. I believe this will happen, though I don't know when or how. I don't always understand God's ways, but I trust Him. He's in charge.*

God has given you some assurances so that you can walk by faith while you're waiting for Him to work. Living by faith and holding on to God's promises gives stability and strength to life, especially when you don't understand what's happening right in front of you.

Ready for some strength training? Let's turn our hearts to one of the most cherished promises in the Bible: Proverbs 3:5–6.

Choose to trust

A lot of people have told me that Proverbs 3:5–6 is their life verse. They know it is a command from God's Word they can live by every day. Is it one of those default-guiding principles in your life? Do you have it underlined in your Bible? Possibly you have it memorized:

Do you say anything like, I know how to fix this. I've been through this before. I'm going to get on this right now. I don't need any help? Yeah, that's not great.

Trust in the LORD with all your heart, and do not lean on your own understanding. In all your ways acknowledge him, and he will make straight your paths.

Proverbs 3:5–6 includes a promise that you've just got to know. Let's take it a phrase at a time.

"Trust in the LORD with all your heart" is obviously an exhortation to deliberately turn away from doubt. When you trust in the Lord *with all your heart*, you're making a tangible choice not to let unbelief trample all over your soul. Instead, you're jumping into walking by faith with both feet—and your heart!

I'd like to think I trust the Lord like that right now, James, but how can I be sure I do?

The next phrase will help you answer that: **"And do not lean on your own understanding."** You can't trust in the Lord with all your heart if you're trying to depend on your own understanding at the same time.

Maybe you know some things. You've been around the block; you know how things work. There's nothing wrong with that. It can be good to have experience and know-how. The question is: Are you leaning on those things when you hit a crisis? Are you placing your confidence in your own ability to get out of tight spots? Do you say anything like, *I know how to fix this. I've been through this before. I'm going to get on this right now. I don't need any help*? Yeah, that's not great. Don't lean on your own understanding. If your trust in God is limited by your understanding of His ways, you will always have a limited trust.

This also applies in your relationships. Let's say you've got a problematic situation in your family. There's friction and tension. Or distance and rebellion. Maybe your son isn't where you wish he would be with God or your mother-in-law isn't very interested in her own spiritual condition. I'm sure you have your own family case studies that leave you feeling helpless. For sure it's not easy, but the way to handle relationships beyond your control is to trust in the Lord with all your heart and do what's right.

I'm going to trust God to honor my choice to love my family. Even when they hurt me; even when they use or neglect me. I trust the Lord to honor my decision to do the right thing.

I'm not going to pay her back for the way she's treating me.

I don't have to be prideful and petty when those I love mistreat me. I can give the matter over to God. I can wait upon Him to work.

(Read Romans 12:16–20; Ephesians 4:2–3, 15–16, 29–32; and 1 Corinthians 13:4–7 for insight and examples of the way that trusting God works in relationships.)

You're not going anywhere good if you doubt God's Word and lean on only what you can see or figure out.

Well, what then? Read on: **"In all your ways acknowledge him."** In every choice, recognize God and factor in His participation. You might be able to handle that situation by yourself, but you don't want to just get out of it, you want to honor God in it. You want to please Him. So in all your ways, you're going to put Him first.

Let's take a practice run at this. Suppose you run into financial problems. Or you lose your job. Or you are beaten out of the big sale you were depending on—not to mention the rising cost of gas and the wild fluctuations on Wall Street. Things are getting so tight that you don't know how you're going to pay the bills.

Humanly speaking, if you were leaning on your own understanding and failing to acknowledge God in the matter, you'd be like, *We're going to tighten the belt around here. No more money to charity. We can't help our little Compassion child anymore; she's going to have to take care of herself. No more juice boxes in the kids' lunches; they can drink from the water fountain. We're not giving to the church anymore either; they seem to be doing fine.*

Now, it's not wrong to be wise in how you spend your money, but if you think you're going to just gut it out, you're leaning on your own understanding. Instead say, *We're going to keep our commitments, including our tithe, and we're going to trust in the Lord with all our hearts. These daunting circumstances are actually a clear opportunity to put trust into action.* We're going to believe that the 90 percent we're left with—with God's help—is more than 100 percent on our own without God. We're not going to get out of this tight spot without Him. So, we're going to acknowledge He's right here in the tight spot with us. We are going to put God first in our lives and trust Him to keep His promises.

Don't you think God knows how much you have? Don't you think God sees your situation? Wasn't it God Himself who said through the prophet in Malachi 3:10, **"Bring the full tithe into the storehouse. . . . And thereby put me to the test . . . if I will not open the windows of heaven for you and pour down for you a blessing until there is no more need?"** *Just try Me on that one,* God says. *Test Me and see if I'm not faithful.* Here's your chance to discover what it means to totally trust Him. Then get ready for the promise that comes at the end of the passage in Proverbs: **"And he will make straight your paths."**

As we've already seen, God makes two kinds of promises—conditional and unconditional. This one is conditional—you've got to do something. You have got to trust in the Lord with all your heart. You have got to acknowledge Him in all of your ways without leaning on your own understanding. If you do your part, God will do His part. **"He will make straight your paths."** The wording I memorized as a kid says, **"He shall direct thy paths"** (KJV). That means He will make your paths smooth—God will make the way passable.

In every person's life, there are a fair number of bumps in the road. There's stuff we have to climb over and a ton of concerns that weigh us down. We each have our own list. There are times when all we can see is the hard road and the heavy load. But the Lord promises that if you trust in Him with all your heart, and that if you do not lean on your own understanding, and that if you acknowledge Him in all your ways, then He will make your paths smooth. *God will pave the way for you.*

There's not much worse than driving gravel roads, potholes, and speed bumps in a dangerously overloaded vehicle! Down with living like that! God promises that He will level the ground in front of you. He'll give you the safest, fastest, smoothest road to the best possible destination.

Wow! That's a great promise—no wonder people treasure this passage!

When you think of it, Proverbs 3:5–6 is really quite a commitment on God's part. There are no illusions here. This is God we're talking about. **"Is anything too hard for the LORD?"** (Genesis 18:14). He can handle anything that's in your path with one hand tied behind His back. A common way we express this is by saying, *God is in control.* The doctrinal term for that is "sovereignty." Every believer should be as familiar with this term as he or she is with breathing.

Sovereignty

I got a great e-mail from my dad recently. At the end he wrote, "Will be in unceasing prayer for you and yours on every front known to me and of course through other fronts that I know little or nothing of, but God my Father knows in full detail and has under His sovereign control." He then added, "I've been in Psalm 103 all this week. Love and kisses, Dad."

My dad is a great believer. He knows all about the sovereignty of God. Since my last book, *When Life Is Hard*, my mom, to whom that book was dedicated, completed her battle with ALS and passed to heaven. During the final days of her painful, debilitating ordeal, my dad was a rock. Watching my mother lose her speech, her swallowing, her motion, until her last moments of communication came only through blinking, my dad stood strongly on the Word of God. As his wife of 54 years suffered greatly, he drew upon a deeply held conviction about the sovereignty of God. He trusted that God's will was the best for him and his wife. That quiet, shining faith became everyone's strength.

If you want to comfort your own heart and also have something to give to another believer, you've got to understand the biblical doctrine of God's sovereignty. No matter what happens or comes our way, we have a God who is in complete control—that's what sovereignty means.

Now how good would the promises of God be if we had to wait and see if He could really do it? God never overpromises or underdelivers. He never has. Why? Because there is nothing too hard for Him. He can do anything. He is in complete control.

God is sovereign over the universe

You say, *He's in control—of what? What do you mean by "everything"?* That's one of those typical questions asked by people who aren't really ready for the answer. It certainly is an issue the Bible responds to fully. In Acts 17, Paul was preaching to some philosophers in Athens, Greece. In verses 24– 25 he said, **"The God who made the world and everything in it, being Lord of heaven and earth, does not live in temples made by man."** God doesn't live in our church buildings. He's not hanging out there all week while you go wherever you go. He **"does not live in temples made by man, nor is he served by human hands, as though he needed anything, since he himself gives to all mankind life and breath and everything."** We may be humbled by the vast reaches of the universe, but God is familiar with every nook, cranny, black hole, and galaxy. He created it all and manages every tiny part of it.

God is sovereign over humanity

Take a deep breath right now. In . . . and out. . . . The capacity to take another breath is a gift from God. Think of the thousands of heartbeats that have kept you alive to this moment—aren't you glad you didn't have to command your heart to contract even a single time?

Continuing in Acts 17, verse 28 says, **"In him we live and move and** have our being." Looking back to verse 26 we read, **"And he made from one man** [Adam] **every nation of mankind to live on all the face of the earth, having determined allotted periods and the boundaries of their dwelling place."** So God is Lord of the countries; Lord of the races; Lord of the governments. And He has a purpose for how He has determined us to live on this earth: **"That they should seek God, in the hope that they might feel their way toward him and find him. Yet he is actually not far from each one of us . . . 'For we are indeed his offspring'"** (vv. 27–28). Paul found in the Athenians' own literature an acknowledgment of God's sovereignty!

> *He's sovereign. He is able to listen to all of our prayers at the same time because He is sovereign.*

You can't make up who God is. It always makes me sad when I hear people say, "Well to me God is . . . such and such." You're already off track. That whole premise is irrelevant. God is who God is no matter what you think. **"Being then God's offspring, we ought not to think that the divine being is like gold or silver or stone, an image formed by the art and imagination of man,"** Paul says in verse 29. You say, "Well, I didn't know that—you mean God doesn't have to be what I imagine Him to be?" In a word, *No.* **"The times of ignorance God overlooked, but now he commands all people everywhere to repent, because he has fixed a day on which he will judge the world in righteousness by a man whom he has appointed** [that's Jesus Christ]**; and of this he has given assurance to all by raising him from the dead"** (v. 30). The arrival, death, and resurrection of Jesus definitely raised the bar of repentance for all of humanity. God will eventually exercise His sovereignty by judgment.

God is so in control that He rules the universe with His feet up. He's not stressed or strained in any way. He's not pacing back and forth. He doesn't wipe sweat from His brow. There is no world problem that stretches Him. God is infinite. He could have made the universe a billion times more complex than it already is. He's God and He is sovereign.

This truth lies behind every one of God's promises. He can be present with us because He's sovereign. He is able to listen to all of our prayers at the same time because He is sovereign. How many thousands of people were out of bed and on their knees last night, calling out to God—and He heard *every one* of us simultaneously. Why? Because He's God and He's sovereign.

Ephesians 1:11 says that God determines **"all things according to the counsel of his will."** We can hope things will happen—but God *makes* things happen. We get our little tasks done as quickly as we can, because we're afraid tomorrow we won't be able to. God doesn't even *think* about stuff like that. He makes it happen on time, every time, with ease.

God is sovereign over our rebellion

Do you remember Jonah? God was like, *You're going to Nineveh and you're going to deliver My message.* And Jonah was like, *I'm not going there and I'm not doing that.* So determined was Jonah's resistance that he booked a cruise going west instead of east, where God had told him to go. So all of a sudden, out of nowhere, **"the LORD sent out a great wind on the sea"** (Jonah 1:4 NKJV). In fact, in Hebrew, that means literally that God *hurled* the storm at him. God was like, "You're going that way, are you? Well try this obstacle on for size." All of a sudden everyone on the boat was afraid for their lives. Jonah admitted that he was the reason for the storm, and the crew made him walk the plank. But was God done with him yet? *No.*

Jonah 1:17 tells us, **"the LORD appointed a great fish to swallow up Jonah."** Jonah prayed to the Lord in the belly of the fish, and he got spit out on dry land. Jonah hadn't even landed and his feet were already moving in the direction where God had told him previously to go, to Nineveh, where he was to call the people to repentance.

In the end, despite His prophet's lackluster performance, God brought a sweeping revival to those wicked people. But Jonah chose to be discouraged and depressed because he didn't think the Ninevites deserved God's mercy. I guess it was going to take more than three days in a fish to knock the pride and rebellion out of Jonah's heart. Jonah was so angry, in fact, that he said, **"O LORD, please take my life from me, for it is better for me to die than to live"** (Jonah 4:3). Now, that's pouting with an attitude! And

God, in His tender love, responded by asking him, "**Do you do well to be angry?**"(4:4) The Lord "**appointed a plant and made it come up over Jonah, that it might be a shade over his head, to save him from his discomfort**" (4:6) and it grew up over Jonah and gave him shade. But, oops, God also sent a worm to gnaw on the plant and it died. Jonah was ticked! Then the Lord came to him and said, "**Is it right for you to be angry about the plant?" And he said, "It is right for me to be angry, even to death!**" (Jonah 4:9 NKJV). Seriously, Jonah? Yet the Lord was so tender and loving toward Him that He went after his heart just as certainly as He had pursued the people of Nineveh. God is sovereign over rebellion.

God is sovereign over sin

When you choose to sin or when the sin of people in your life affects you, God is sovereign over that too. Think of Joseph. God had given him some big dreams for his life, but his brothers' sinful acts seemed to take him far from them. If you remember, Joseph's brothers deceived him, then beat him, stripped him, and sold him as a slave into Egypt. (You can read Joseph's story starting in Genesis 37.)

Joseph's story repeatedly took hard left turns. He ended up in Egypt, trying to honor God with his life; trying to trust the Lord; making decisions of faith; not leaning on his own understanding. But even then, he was unfairly harassed, falsely accused, and then unjustly thrown into prison. It seemed like his days were over, but again, God was in control.

Years later, still in prison, Joseph was working hard, trusting the Lord, still believing God's ways were best, and not leaning on human wisdom— and it seemed like he was finally going to catch a break. But this time it was his new friends who betrayed him. They forgot about him stuck in the dungeon, and again his future looked grim. Every chapter in Joseph's story seems to have had some kind of pit in it! But then God stepped in and demonstrated in amazing detail how He is sovereign over the sins of Joseph's brothers and false accusers and betraying friends.

In the end, Joseph was elevated to a position of authority in a foreign land. Even Pharaoh recognized God's hand on Joseph's life and said to his servants: **"Can we find a man like this, in whom is the Spirit of God?"** (Genesis 41:38). It just so happened that in God's timing, Joseph's brothers soon stood before him with their hands out, asking for bread. Nobody except God could have orchestrated a story with so many twists. You can imagine how terrified Joseph's brothers were when they realized it was "Little Joe" they had abused years earlier before whom they now bowed. But Joseph knew about the sovereignty of God. He looked them in the eyes and said, **"You meant evil against me, but God meant it for good"** (Genesis 50:20). That is an awesome truth: God can use even the sin of other people to accomplish His purposes in your life!

God is sovereign over world events

The story of Esther is another incredible testimony as to how God orchestrates history. In the telling of this historical account, under divine inspiration, the author chose not to mention God's name. But don't miss God's fingerprints all over the events, lining up people and circumstances in perfect timing to preserve His people and advance His agenda.

This episode of epic proportions in real life shows God winning over evil. Satan's tool was a man named Haman, who, not surprisingly, hated God's people. He wielded his power and influence with the king and plotted to legalize a plan that would annihilate the Jews. The Jews were helpless against the law, except that in God's plan, two Jewish people stood in Haman's way. The first was Mordecai, who faithfully held his ground and completely enraged Haman. The second was Esther, Mordecai's niece. You can read the full details in the biblical record entitled Esther.

Esther was chosen to be in the king's harem and because of her God-given beauty was eventually named the queen. But she kept secret the fact that she was a Jew. When Haman's heinous plot became law, Mordecai saw God's plan right away and appealed to Esther to take a stand for her people by influencing the king. But when Esther hesitated, fearing repercussions if the king didn't receive her well, Mordecai gave her a great lesson in God's sovereignty. He said, **"Do not think to yourself that in the king's palace you will escape any more than all the other Jews. For if you keep silent** at this time, relief and deliverance will rise for the Jews from another place, but you and your father's house will perish" (Esther 4:13–14a). *God will have His way. If you don't do it, He'll find someone who will.* No matter what, God's purposes will be accomplished.

Mordecai continued, **"And who knows whether you have not come to the kingdom for such a time as this?"** (Esther 4:14b). All the heartbreaking events of Esther's life, all that she had to endure brought her to that place in history. God knew what He was doing.

Does that truth speak to you today? Look back at your life from where you stand today. Do you see God's sovereign hand directing the circumstances and relationships and events of years past? There has been nothing that others have done that could thwart God's plan for your life. No circumstance, near or far, can change what God purposes to do. In fact, the events that have frustrated, hurt, and derailed your plans may be some of the biggest parts of God's plans for you—even more obvious than His blessings. Consider reevaluating your painful memories in the light of God's sovereignty. What has He been bringing out in you all along the way?

Proverbs 16:33 affirms God's control when it says, **"The lot is cast into the lap, but its every decision is from the LORD."**

We can be confident in God's sovereignty

Let's return to Hebrews 6:18 for encouragement: **"So that by two unchangeable things, in which it is impossible for God to lie, we who have fled for refuge might have strong encouragement to hold fast to the hope set before us."** Let's continue to verse 19 this time: **"We have this as a sure and steadfast anchor of the soul."**

Wow. Read that again. We have a refuge. We have an attachment point for our soul. When the waves are crazy high and the wind whips strong and cold across your face and you don't know what's going to happen, you have an anchor. You have the assurance that God is in control and He has made you some promises. You don't know when those promises will happen, but you can be sure they will. That kind of assurance will settle your heart right down.

Trust God with all of your heart. Don't lean on your own understanding. Refuse to take your cues from what life looks like right now. Instead, acknowledge Him in all of your ways and He will pave the path for you.

Father, thank You that You are able to accomplish what concerns me today (Psalm 138:8). You are able to do exceedingly abundantly above all that we ask or think (Ephesians 3:20). You are able because You are sovereign. There is nothing too hard for You. Continue to engrave upon my heart the reality that I am to walk by faith. I believe what Your Word says, that You have made some exceedingly great and precious promises. Seal these promises to my heart. Don't let the enemy snatch away this seed that You have sown, but let my life reflect the stability of knowing that You see and know and are at work on my behalf. Thank You that You are in control. In Jesus' strong name, Amen.

GOD'S PROMISES ARE AN ASSURANCE GOD GIVES HIS PEOPLE SO
THEY CAN WALK BY FAITH WHILE THEY WAIT FOR HIM TO WORK.

Read Psalm 37. What assurances of God's promises do you see in this psalm? How do the different ways God protects and provides for His children described here strengthen your faith in His character?

Meditate on the directives of Psalm 37:1–7. How do these help you get from the day you understand God's promise through the days of faith until the day He fulfills His promise? For each one, identify at least one specific area in your life where that command applies right now.

- *Fret not yourself because of evildoers; be not envious of wrongdoers!* (v. 1)
- *Trust in the Lord, and do good; dwell in the land and befriend faithfulness.* (v. 3)
- *Delight yourself in the Lord, and he will give you the desires of your heart.* (v. 4)
- *Commit your way to the Lord; trust in him, and he will act.* (v. 5)
- *Be still before the Lord and wait patiently for him.* (v. 7)

KNOW BY HEART
Proverbs 3:5–6

Trust in the Lord with all your heart, and do not lean on your own understanding. In all your ways acknowledge him, and he will make straight your paths.

[THEOLOGY OF A PROMISE]

God is a Promiser by nature.

God keeps all of His promises.

God wants us to test His promises.

GOD WANTS US TO TEST HIS PROMISES.

As a pastor, I've had an up-close-and-personal view of hundreds of weddings. I could tell you all kinds of stories about them, from silly to touching to tragic. The one thing they all have in common is the promise the bride and groom make to each other, their vows. In their own words and ways, weddings are about promises:

For better or for worse, for richer or poorer, in sickness and in health, till death do us part.

To the young, these vows are voiced with doe-eyed infatuation, and sound noble and grand. Ask anyone married for more than a month and they'll tell you that these promises are downright hard to keep. You want to be true to them, but you honestly hope you won't ever be tested.

You promise, *for better or for worse*, but which are you hoping for? *Better!*

You promise, *for richer or poor*, but you're counting on for richer.

You promise, *in sickness and in health*, but you mean, "Well, I hope you're not going to be sick, but if it comes to that, I'll try to be there for you."

You don't want it to come to any of these tests, but if it does, you're ready—you've given your word.

You've promised.

That's where we're different from God. He already knows what the difficulties will be, but He makes His promise anyway! He *expects* you to be at a crossroads where you *have* to lean on Him; where you *must* rest on His promises; and where you *are ready* to claim them, hold them, and treasure them in your heart. God flat out *wants* you to test His promises.

I was in my study this week when I had one of those *aha!* experiences. It was like I was hearing for the first time that *God wants me to test His promises.* He wants me to get out where the ice is thin and the wind is howling and experience His holding me up.

Not only does God want you to test His promises, but He is ordering the circumstances of your life in such a way that you *will have* to trust Him. Every single person who knows and loves the Lord will experience times when they have no other option but to put God's promises to the test. God is going to make sure the crisis happens.

Psalm 119:140 says, **"Your promise is well tried, and your servant loves it."** I don't love the fact that I get to test His promises so much as I love the fact that God *wants* me to test Him. He's so settled and confident in His commitment to me that He says, *Go ahead—try Me!* And every time I do test Him, God proves Himself true.

God's Promises Never Fail

Just to prove this point, let's take another trip through Scripture looking for proof from just a few of the times God has delivered big time on a promise He made:

Proof #1: The children of Israel in the wilderness, Joshua 21:45

After the children of Israel had exited Egypt, wandered through the wilderness, and finally conquered the Promised Land, Joshua 21:45 testifies that, **"Not one word of all the good promises that the LORD had made to the house of Israel had failed; all came to pass."**

- Forty years of wilderness, five million people to protect and care for— *done.*
- How many of God's promises failed? Not one of them.
- How many came to pass? All of them.

Between Egypt and Jericho, God ensured that every promise got tested. Everything He said they had to trust, and every single one of His words proved true. God made sure of it.

Proof #2: Solomon in the temple, 1 Kings 8:56

A couple hundred years later, with Israel in the Promised Land, Solomon was dedicating the temple and he again affirmed the promises of God. First Kings 8:56 says, **"Blessed be the LORD who has given rest to His people, according to all that he promised. Not one word has failed of all his good promise, which he spoke by Moses his servant."**

- How many words failed? *Not one!*
- Every single syllable God spoke came to pass.

Solomon looked back and confirmed that there wasn't one instance when anyone could say, *Well, that didn't turn out quite like what He said.* History unfolded exactly as God had declared it would. God made it so that His people would have to test it; and **"not one word has failed."**

Proof #3: My life and yours, Deuteronomy 11:26–28

I've been preaching for more than twenty years, and I've never said this till now: My life is proof of the Word of God. Yours is too. There is a massive experiment under way in which we all are participating. Is God's Word true? Does it bear itself out in your life?

- If you obey, you're going to get blessed. Your life is proof of that promise.
- If you disobey, you're going to get consequences. Your life is a proof of that reality.

In its totality, God's Word is a bunch of promises and consequences. God says in Deuteronomy 11:26–28, **"See, I am setting before you today a blessing and a curse: the blessing, if you obey the commandments of the LORD your God, . . . and the curse, if you do not obey the commandments of the LORD your God."** One way or another, we prove the Word of God. It's always been this way.

Scripture is on the line right now in your life. By one outcome or another, the Word of God is going to be proven true in your life.

Psalm 33:11 offers this incredible affirmation: **"The counsel of the LORD stands forever, the plans of his heart to all generations."** Isaiah 40:8 tells us that people are like the grass. We wither and fade like last season's wildflowers, **"but the word of our God will stand forever."** Children and grandchildren will come and go, but God's Word will still be around. Other generations will prove the promises or the judgments of God just like our lives do.

Believe the promises: get blessed. Disobey the commands: get consequences.

Our lives are proof of the Word of God.

But aren't we told: "Don't put God to the test"?

Now James, you're telling us that God invites us to test His promises, but doesn't Jesus tell Satan in Matthew 4:7 that **"You shall not put the Lord your God to the test"**? What does *that* mean?

Good question; and I'm glad for the chance to clarify. Jesus' warning to not put God to the test means two things:

#1. Don't act foolishly and expect God to bail you out.

In Matthew 4, Satan was tempting Jesus to jump from the pinnacle of the temple to see if God would send angels to catch Him. Sounds like something junior-high boys do rather than the Son of God. If Jesus had fallen for that satanic ploy, He would not only have been making a rash move, He would actually be revealing doubt about His own identity! The dare from the devil was, "If you are the Son of God . . ." Jesus wasn't tempted to prove something He already knew.

Some people take one of God's promises and push it to the limit. Take for instance His promise to meet our needs in Philippians 4:19, **"And my God will supply every need of yours according to his riches in glory in Christ Jesus."** God promises that as you seek Him first (Matthew 6:33), you're never going to lack for the basic provisions of life—food, shelter, and clothing. One way or another, God's going to take care of that. Some people twist His promise and say, "Well then, let's sell the house. Let's give away all of our money. Torch the car, and let's go sit in a field. Take care of me *now*, God!" Jesus was saying, *Don't act foolishly like that and then expect God to bail you out.*

Do people really do that? you might wonder. I wish we could ask Madeline

Kara Neumann, an eleven-year-old girl from Wisconsin, but we can't ask her because she died. She had what should have been an easily treatable form of diabetes, but her parents decided that they would pray for her rather than get her medical treatment. When she didn't get well on prayer alone, they got more people to pray for her. The police chief reported that when they went to the house after Madeline died, her mother was saying that they expected God to raise her from the dead. Tragic.

Don't act foolishly and expect God to bail you out. Is prayer important? Of course it is. But do everything *you* can do and then trust God to do what you cannot do. Every day of the week for nearly forty years, God miraculously provided His people with manna—but they still had to go out and pick it up!

#2. Don't act willfully and provoke God to judge you for rebellion and ungratefulness.

When Jesus responded to Satan in Matthew 4, he was quoting Deuteronomy 6:16: **"You shall not put the LORD your God to the test, as you tested him at Massah."**

What happened at Massah? The word "Massah" translates to "testing." This is a significant location mentioned in Exodus 17. God had brought the children of Israel out of Egypt, out of slavery, and out of harm's way. He fed them every day with bread from heaven. Yet one day the group woke up and went ballistic because there was a temporary water shortage. Moses was afraid for his life as the people turned against God. They shook their fists and said, "You're evil, God! You can't be trusted. You brought us out here to kill us unless You give us water right now!"

Here's a warning: Do not *ever* do that. Don't disregard every good thing He has done for you and turn rebellious and ungrateful and whine, "If You don't fix this situation, You're not God. You don't care about me." Don't put it all on the line over one thing and demand God work right now. When we try this, we're not depending on God so much as we are trying to demonstrate just how much influence we have with Him. Ordering God around is not going to turn things around for you.

Don't *ever* say something like, "Well if there really is a God, then let Him strike me dead right now." You might think you're okay if you survive the next five minutes, but you don't know what's coming your way later for so wrongfully putting God to the test.

Don't make God say, **Enough!**

I recently read yet another story of a minister's moral collapse. He was an associate pastor on the staff of a Bible-believing, gospel-preaching church. The staff was understandably upset at their colleague's failure. The senior pastor is a good friend of mine and I said to him on the phone, "God wanted this to come out. He doesn't want sin covered and hidden. He brings it out in the open so it'll get dealt with no matter how painful it is."

Tragically more than twenty years ago, that same church experienced a senior pastor who was serially unfaithful to his wife. When it all came out, he wouldn't repent or even acknowledge his sin, and it split the church.

All the good that God had done for this man wasn't enough to bring him to repentance. One day that very fit and healthy man was out jogging and down he went—dead. Something exploded in his brain and God took him. *Enough of that!* it seems God said.

Don't put God in that situation. Don't provoke Him with ungratefulness and rebellion. Don't act foolishly and expect Him to bail you out. That's what **"You shall not put the Lord your God to the test"** means. It most certainly does not mean "Don't test God's promises." God wants us to experience personally that what He promises is true.

Test the promises of God

In the city where I grew up there was a park that had a big lake in the middle of hundreds of acres of pine trees. In the winter my brothers and I would skate on the frozen lake. Unless you live in "cold country," you may not know that lakes freeze from the center out. The thickest ice is in the middle, and the thinnest ice is near shore. When the ice starts to melt, there might be water around the edge of the lake, but the center can still hold you up.

Well, we always wanted to skate as long during the winter season as we possibly could. So when the weather turned warmer, we would experiment with the ice. We'd try to jump over the icy-water mix around the outside and land farther from shore, then strap our skates on and go. We would use the same tactic getting off the ice, jumping over the water to get to land. I got a lot of "soakers" getting that feat accomplished. It wasn't very deep at the edge, but you could never tell exactly where the ice would hold you up.

Now think about the promises of God. He wants us to get out on the ice and test His Word. He wants us to be sure from experience that it will hold us up. God wants us to rest our lives on His promises. Keeping one foot firmly anchored to shore while the other cautiously reaches out to stand on the promises is likely to result in wet feet. You're never sure if what held you up was the foot on the edge where your own understanding and resources reside or out on the ice, where only God's promises are sustaining your weight. God wants us to believe His promises, depend on them, and get out on the ice and skate.

"Will You really be with me, God? Is it right that I don't fear?" *Yes, I am with you! You don't have to fear.*

"Is it true that I don't have to doubt because You're in control?" *Yes, it's true.*

These are the promises of God.

Let's review our theology of a promise so far:
- God is a Promiser by nature.
- God keeps all of His promises.
- Now, God wants you to test His promises.

*The more you go through in life, the deeper your
love for the Lord can grow.*

You test His promises and find Him good and faithful.

He knows what He is doing. He is worthy of every moment of trust.

With this third promise comes a deeper level of commitment on our part: I will not despair, because God is always good. No matter what the degree of our need, God supplies a promise that meets that need and beyond. This is because, to us the picture from our theological note, sometimes life is all about the fun of skating and other times it's about the fear of the ice cracking under our feet.

Promise #1 tells us, "God is with me," and kind of begs the question, *Fine. I get it. He's with me, but what is He doing?* Promise #2 assures us that God is in control. *Well, that's all good. God is steering the canoe and I'm in the front paddling, but hang on—we're headed for the falls!* And that's when we need Promise #3: God is always good.

With this third promise, we get to God's heart. Not only is He with me; not only is He sovereign and ordering the circumstances of my life, but God is good. God's goodness is the ultimate rescue net under all of life's experiences. No matter what you are facing today, soon you will see, and say, and sing, "God is so good."

The goodness of God is stamped all over Scripture. Psalm 27:13 says,

"I would have despaired unless I had believed that I would see the goodness of the LORD in the land of the living" (NASB). I love David's honesty. Here was the only man called **"a man after [God's] own heart"** (1 Samuel 13:14), anointed by Samuel to be king of Israel, a giant-slayer, but no stranger to suffering, saying, "I would have lost it; I would have melted down if I had not believed. . . ."

The Bleakness of Despair

Despair is a place that you don't want *any*one to go. You don't even want people you don't like to go there. People who go there often don't come back. Despair is an utterly and enduringly dark place.

When I was a kid, our family spent summer holidays traveling all over Canada and the U. S., pulling our little camper trailer behind our car. One of the places I vividly remember visiting was Carlsbad Caverns. I remember hiking down, down, down, into the deepest tunnels, more than 1,600 feet into the earth. The deeper we went, the darker and damper it got. Though the New Mexican desert floor sweltered above us, we got so cold and clammy down there that we were thankful for a sweater. I remember fearing how scary it would be if the electricity went off and the artificial light and air circulation shut down while we were deep in the caverns.

That's the picture that comes to mind when I think of despair. It's that crushing awareness that you are deep down, in a damp, dark cave, far from sunshine or warmth. No light. No air. No hope. Alone. Nobody wants to go to despair.

One dictionary defines *despair* as "destitute of positive expectations." If you're in despair, you can't see anything good in your future.

You have no idea how life could improve.

You have no words to pray.

You can't recall a better time because there isn't one. That memory or place is gone.

You can't remove the circumstances because the opportunity has vanished.

You can't retrieve any level of relationship because the person has left.

You can't do it over because the time has passed.

If you focus on the dark, the deep, and the damp, you're traveling downward into despair.

Accelerants for despair

Maybe it's a guy thing, but I love to barbeque. We have a gas barbeque now, but I sort of miss the charcoal days, especially that volatile lighter fluid you squirt on the charcoal. Since I was a kid I've loved to just spray the charcoal and flick a match and *pphhhffff*—up go the flames. It's called an "accelerant" for a good reason. A small flicker of flame erupts into a raging fire in almost no time at all. Well, there's a lesson in that. Let me tell you three things that are accelerants for despair. Watch out for these:

Surprise: *I did not see this coming. Everything was going great and BAM! I was laid flat.* A heart attack. A car accident. A betrayal—and suddenly life turns on a dime. No time to brace yourself. Surprise will take you quickly to despair.

Severity: You don't despair over a parking ticket. You wouldn't even despair over losing a job, but you very well may find cause for despair over losing a cherished career—the pianist losing dexterity; the artist losing sight; the athlete losing mobility; the teacher losing her voice; or something else, like a parent losing a child. A severe loss delivers an invitation to despair.

Settledness: Despair concludes that something bad is irreversible. The opportunity is gone. The relationship is over. The train has left the station and is never coming back.

Buying into any of these three mind-sets is like pouring accelerant on your despair. Better to step away from the flame and get God's perspective on the problem.

David knew better; He heard the tempter's voice telling him to give up but he instead turned his eyes toward God. **"I would have despaired unless I had believed."** *I could have—I would have—except I chose to believe in God.*

Get hold of God's promises

Instead of lighting that match, David fired up his confidence in a promise-keeping God. You and I need to do the same. We need to get hold of some promises. People will say, *I don't know how she can be so strong through this . . .* and *How can he just keep going with everything that's happening?*

I'll tell you how—we fix our hope on our promise-keeping God. Here's our job:

Exodus 14:13–14 says, **"Stand firm, and see the salvation of the LORD. . . . The LORD will fight for you, and you have only to be silent."**

Your job is to button it up. Don't inflame the situation with stupid talk. Keep your mouth shut and hold on to the promises.

> *I'm still going to be alive on terra firma when I see God's goodness.*

Isaiah 30:15 says, **"In quietness and in trust shall be your strength."**

Psalm 46:10 reminds us to **"Be still, and know that I am God."** When you come to the place where you can't do anything else, you must stand still and believe. We think that's the worst possible place to be, but God loves it when we're there. When you can't do anything, let God do it all.

"I would have despaired unless I had believed that I would see the goodness of the LORD in the land of the living."

Look closely at the God you're trusting in. Notice the phrase, **"that I would see."** David believed that he was going to witness God's work. He wasn't just going to hear about it; he was going to see God's goodness with his own eyes.

Now think about the last phrase in the verse—**"in the land of the living."** *I'm going to see it in my lifetime. This is no front-row-seat-in-heaven thing, man! I'm still going to be alive on terra firma when I see God's goodness.*

Do you have faith to believe that? *I'm going to see my daughter come home. I'm going to see my spouse turn back to God. I'm going to see my career turn in a better direction. I'm going to get a good report from the doctor.* The life of faith doesn't know *how* it's going to happen; it simply maintains the perspective that with God, good outcomes are my future!

The School of Suffering

When our son Luke was three years old, we would ask him, *What do you want to be when you grow up?*

And he would answer, *A preacher of the gospel of Jesus Christ!*

There were days when I wondered about that childhood dream. There were even days when I told him to plan on some other career. But God has been at work in his life and is already using him in ministry. Luke graduated from Moody Bible Institute with his college degree; we are as proud as we can be.

But the reality is that a lot of people graduate from college. There's another school, however, that Luke will need to attend multiple times in his walk with Christ. It's called "the school of suffering." Every one of God's children enroll; very few truly graduate. How many times have I thought I was done with this school only to be taken back for another term.

I've already told you how I love to study the lives of pastors in generations past. I think very highly of A. W. Tozer. If you read nothing else of his, you must get these two books under your nose: *The Pursuit of God* and *The Knowledge of the Holy*. They will open a world of intimacy with God that you may never have known existed. Make a note to read one of these little volumes—right after you're done with this book!

As a teenager on his way home from work at a tire company, Tozer overheard a street preacher say: "If you don't know how to be saved . . . just call on God." When he got home, he climbed into his parents' attic, and did what the preacher said. He immersed himself in God's Word. Five years after coming to Christ in faith and repentance, Tozer accepted an offer to pastor his first church. This began many years of ministry, with thirty of them (1928 to 1959) on the south side of Chicago.

Tozer was no stranger to suffering. Two sons were wounded in World War II. The people in his church turned hostile toward him. His own broken health laid him up for weeks at a time. I could go on and on. One of God's greatest saints was a graduate student in "the school of suffering." But his experiences with God's faithfulness flavor everything he wrote.

When our church moved into the large corporate center that had been given to us (another outrageous testimony of God's goodness), we made an amazing discovery. In a random filing cabinet drawer buried beneath boxes and trash, we found a stack of paper three inches thick, bound together with rubber bands. They were copies of A. W. Tozer's last ten years of sermon outlines. We have no idea how they came to be in that filing cabinet. I have spent protracted time reading through these reams of Tozer's original preaching notes. What I see is that the quality of his ministry came from the depth of his suffering. God kept taking him back again and again to that school nobody wants to attend. Viewing his life in retrospect, you see that the seeds of suffering produced the abundant fruit in his work.

So here are a few things about the goodness of God that Tozer learned. I see these lessons in my own life, and I hope you are learning them too. Let's do a flyby of Scripture that boasts in the goodness of the Lord.

God's goodness is something He wants us to experience

Psalm 34:8 invites us to **"taste and see that the LORD is good."** I'm a bigtime taster. If I'm ever around you at meal time, guard your plate. I admit I like to sample. To me, friends share food; that's intimacy. People who are territorial about the helpings on their plates sometimes get a little leery when I show up, but the good news is that God is totally on that program. He's like, "*Taste!* Sample and see. Find out for yourself that I am good." God's goodness is something that He wants us to experience.

God's goodness is the eventual conclusion of every generation of His children

You might not think it now, but if you're one of God's children, you're going to figure it out by the end of your life—God is good. Before your last day, "God is good" will come from your lips. I don't know what He's going to have to take you through to get you to that place, but eventually your value system will be set up in such a way that you say, "The Lord does all things well—and good!" Everything that He allowed, everything He withheld, every difficult season, every stretching circumstance, He meant for good.

His disposition is kindness. His default action is for your benefit. He's good! And someday, you will taste it!

Psalm 100:5 says, **"For the LORD is good; his steadfast love endures forever, and his faithfulness to all generations."** Every generation learns the truth—God's goodness is something He wants us to experience. It flows to us as **steadfast love** and **faithfulness** and is present in everything that He does.

God's goodness is all over what He does

Psalm 145:9 says, **"The LORD is good to all, and his mercy is over all that he has made."** I haven't found God to be superfast in answering questions like, *Why did You allow this, God?* or *When will this end?* But I do believe His mercy or His kindness is over all that He is doing.

God's goodness may not be immediately obvious

Lamentations 3:25 says, **"The LORD is good to those who wait for him."** But if you're like, "I've got to see it now! God; You've got like ten days to show me that You're good or I am out of here!" That's not going to work out very well for you. God doesn't respond to bullying. He's not shaking and saying, *Wow. We'd better go over and help him because he could leave.* That's not how it works. Even His timetable is good, but we can only see this after events have transpired. Our prayer must be, "Father, I'm waiting for You because I know You are good in *what* You do and in *when* You do it!"

God's goodness is a refuge, and He is aware of the people who find it

I don't know what you know about the goodness of the Lord, but God knows what you know, and what you're discovering about Him. Nahum 1:7 says, **"The LORD is good, a stronghold in the day of trouble; he knows those who take refuge in him."**

As God watches us live our lives, He points to you and says, "She's trusting," or "He's not," and "He's trusting a bit," and "She did last Thursday." He knows those who are taking His promises to heart. He's proving the Word of God in our lives. He knows the people who are resting in and the people who are resisting His promises. **Stronghold** is what God's goodness looks like to the enemy on the outside; **refuge** is what God's goodness looks like to us on the inside. **He knows** in this verse doesn't just mean *He recognizes*; it also means *He draws near in intimate fellowship when we protect ourselves within His character.*

We grow in our awareness of God's goodness

Dick Roos was one of the original eighteen people who started our church. We had a lot of faith in those early years. We had to—we weren't really sure if anyone would come to our first services. You can't tell by the size of the acorn how large a tree is hidden inside.

Dick had childhood-onset diabetes. In the early 1990s, he got pretty sick and had a kidney and pancreas transplant, but his body was unable to adapt to the new organs. For weeks we prayed fervently that God would heal him; that God would spare him. I was away working on my doctoral thesis in the summer of 1994 when I got word that Dick had passed away. This was the first time a major leader in our church had died. During the days that Dick was fading I tried to help his wife Janet see God's goodness, but things were just too dark then.

Of course I flew home to preach at his funeral but I remember feeling very unsatisfied with the words that I had to say to this young widow. I felt like I was digging for meaningful words that would comfort her heart but came up empty.

A couple weeks after Dick went to heaven, I remember Janet calmly saying to me, "You know, James. God is good."

I wondered, *How could she say that?* I was still struggling with it all myself. My mind agreed with her, but my heart was having a hard time getting with the program. She was certainly grieving the loss of her life companion, and yet she was able to claim God's merciful hand in her circumstances. Her settled hope was as real as her pain and I was deeply convicted to get my heart to the same conclusion.

With the years I've come to understand that when you're suffering, your nose is up against a wall and you can't see anything but brick. You don't recognize God's goodness. As the years go by, and you take a step backward and then another step and another, and you get more time and separation from your crisis, you begin to make out the mural that is painted on the wall. Eventually

> God has a plan for your *life*. He's got some objectives He's working out.

you can see that your pain was part of a much larger picture that God was carefully painting.

God's mercies have been obvious in Janet's life. A couple of years went by, and she met and married a man named Paul. He adopted her two girls and they've had another daughter. They're happy and blessed and serving the Lord. She was right in holding on to God's promises.

God has a plan for *your* life. He's got some objectives He's working out.

When Dick died, Janet testified to the goodness of God—but she had said it was 98 percent by faith at the time. Only a small part of her conviction was fact-based. Only in time did her faith become sight and her eyes gaze upon the goodness of God's promises. Yet when God's goodness was really hard to see, she still embraced it by faith. Give your trial time, walk by faith, hold on to the promises, and believe that in your lifetime you'll see God's goodness, and you will.

Janet reminded me recently of the verse that I gave her during that valley through the shadow of death. When I felt like I had so little to say, I gave her one of my favorite promises, Jeremiah 29:11: **"For I know the plans I have for you, declares the LORD, plans for welfare and not for evil, to give you a future and a hope."** It turns out that God had a lot to tell her when I was at a loss for words!

God's Plans Are Good

God has some plans—for you. God instructed the prophet Jeremiah to write this message to the nation of Israel while they were in exile in a foreign country. Everything around them was unfamiliar, and their departing memories of the Promised Land were pictures of utter devastation. There wasn't much to go back to except the broken walls of Jerusalem and the glorious temple in ruins. Yet, when they were far from home God came toward them and said, "This isn't going to change right away. You're going to be here for a while, but I have not left you alone. Wait on Me."

Then He promised in Jeremiah 29:11, **"For I know the plans I have for you."** The phrase, "I know" is emphatic. It's more like, "*I know that I know* the plans that I have for you—and these are well thought-out plans, too." Do you doubt that God has plans for you? You may be stuck in a situation that has no visible or discernible exit. *How could this possibly get you to a better place?*

God has a plan for *your* life. He's got some objectives He's working out. We get stuck in the bottomless vortex of *Who should I marry?* and *Where will I live?* and *What about a job?* But God's plans are not so much about those details as they are about developing your character and embracing the righteousness that He's installing in your life. God knows that if He can get that into you, everything else will sort itself out.

It gives me great comfort to know that God knows His plans for my life, but I would really love to get a hint at them too. Do you know what I mean? *Can I know the plans He has for me? And if God knows, why isn't He telling me?* The tension isn't, "Does God know?" but, "I want to know!" Yet I know that God doesn't feel any tension at all. He never apologizes for saying, "I know, but I'm not going to let you know—until later."

He does give us hints, however. Here are some general categories that describe the plan God has for you.

First of all, it's a plan for **"welfare."** The Hebrew word is *shalom*, meaning "the complete state of well-being, fulfillment, prosperity, peace." As God looks down the telescope of time, His eternal plans are for your total well-being. Everything is going to work out for you. That's your end story. That's where it's all headed for the child of God. Sure, you can mess things up a little bit if you insist on doing things your own way, but you'll never derail His plans. He sees where the tracks are going and makes sure you get to the station!

His plans are **"not for evil."** If you're living in sin, that is not God's plan for your life. If someone in your family is living in sin, you can tell him or her confidently that their choices are not what God wants for them. People who are determined to prove they can live at cross-purposes with God's plans will pay too high a price for their experiment. God's plans take us away from evil; our plans take us smack into the middle of it! Our plans will never work out for good; God's plans always work out for good!

I love the next words, which summarize God's plan: **"to give you a future."** If you were to ask the Lord, "Tell me what You want to do with my life." *Well it's to give you a future.* Think of it…*You have a future*—immediately and eternally. God knows all about it and it's incredible.

Another great phrase follows: **"and a hope."** What kind of future is in God's plan? A good one to which you can look forward. That's why you can hope. The biblical definition of "hope" is a "confident expectation of something better tomorrow." We all know the disappointments that come when we base an-

> *He's not the cause of evil, but He is the solution. His purposes will be accomplished.*

ticipation on what we and other humans can deliver. God will never have a problem delivering! It doesn't matter what has happened, better things are coming. God's plan produces hope in me.

To Remember in Any Trial

Anyone who has been through a deep valley and rested on the promises of God has likely also embraced Romans 8:28: **"And we know that for those who love God all things work together for good, for those who are called according to his purpose."** You could comfort a Christian with just the reference. Just say, *Going through a hard time?—Romans 8:28—*and most would know what you mean.

Why is this passage so comforting? It begins with the words, **"And we know."** We don't merely *think*; we don't merely *wonder*; we *know*.

The word *know* communicates experiential knowledge—the kind that comes from life. You didn't go to church or to college to have this explained to you. You didn't Google the answer. You know only because you've been through it. Over time you've come to accept something that only those who love God know: He works things out for good. This is one of those tried and definitely true promises in God's Word about how He works!

Only God's children—those who have turned from their sin and embraced Christ by faith; those who are increasingly learning how to love God more and more—understand the great promise of this verse. Only those who have tested the promises of God and proven once again His faithful love know. As I mentioned back in the introduction, these promises of God carried my wife and me through the darkest days of our lives.

As I prepared the truths on these pages, I woke up in the middle of the night. While there have been times when fears have descended like a cold cloud in those night hours, this time I lay in bed and talked with the Lord. I told Him how much I loved Him. I didn't worry about counting sheep; I was having an intimate conversation with my Shepherd. Have you also found that the more you go through, the more you love the Lord? This experience came during the worst and lowest time of my life, when all we had was our faith in God's promises. Then, when you test His promises you find Him to be so good and faithful. He is *with* you. God knows what He is doing. He is worthy of every moment of trust.

Have life's difficulties caught you off guard? Do you wonder today if God is good? If He wasn't going to use that hard thing for your good, it wouldn't have happened. He had to sign off on every single thing that touches your life (He's sovereign, remember?). If He let it happen, He's going to use it for good. That's not to say He wanted it; He's not the cause of evil, but He is the solution. He's the master chess player who takes every move we make or someone else makes and strategizes the next move to ensure His purposes are accomplished.

I have come to realize over time that the ultimate good of Romans 8:28 is not "my little blueprint for life;" the ultimate good is God's blueprint for the universe and my place in it. I'm committed to God's purposes. I want His will to be fulfilled and His kingdom to advance. I want to be a part of that grand plan. Being on board with God's objectives means I understand that this is not about me.

I believe God is working all things together for the good of those who love Him; for the good of those who are the called according to His purpose.

—⊙✎⊙—

Father, I feel faith rising in me as I believe Your Word. Your Word is true. By Your grace, I will not despair. I believe that I will see the goodness of the Lord in the land of the living. I believe that You have plans for me for wholeness and not for evil. I believe that You have a future and a hope for me. I believe that You are working all things together for the good of those who love You. Lord, Your promises are exceedingly great and precious to me. I say by faith that You are good. In Jesus' name, Amen.

Rehearse in your mind the situations in your life right now that are "in process." They may be difficult, or unknown, or not going as you would dream they would. They're the big things, the situations that keep you up at night. With those circumstances in mind, say by faith:

Even though today _____ (name the situation), I will not despair because I believe God is good and that He will work all things together for my good and His glory.

To further commit this to faith, write out this statement (with as many circumstances as you are currently facing) on a 3 x 5 card and put it in a place where you will see it often—in your Bible, on the car dash, etc. Believe God's promise to you is true and you will trust Him.

KNOW BY HEART
Romans 8:28

And we know that for those who love God all things work together for good, for those who are called according to his purpose.

[THEOLOGY OF A PROMISE]

God is a Promiser by nature.

God keeps all of His promises.

God wants us to test His promises.

God's promises are activated by faith.

GOD'S PROMISES ARE ACTIVATED BY FAITH.

I grew up going to my grandma's house. She used to have a small ceramic loaf of bread on the center of the kitchen table. In it was a stack of little cards, and on those small rectangles were printed promises from the Bible. Sometimes before my grandfather would pray for the meal, he'd say, "Let's read a promise," and he'd take a card out and read it. I grew up hearing these promises, but I never really understood how they worked.

I didn't get the fact that it is in God's nature to promise and that God's whole relationship with us is carried out in line with His promises. God gives us His promises to get through the painful circumstances of life. I didn't understand how the promises worked—until I went through a time when the promises became my lifeline.

The many, many trials from my cancer to our church conflicts—to the heavy burdens we carried for our children (all detailed in *When Life Is Hard*) were the crucible that forged our deeper understanding of God's promises. Those promises became to us what Peter describes as "exceedingly great and precious" (2 Peter 1:4). God's promises may not seem great until we need them. We may not consider them precious until they're proven in the heat and pressure of pain. Until we put all of our weight on them and they hold us up, we don't get it. But test them and they'll always prove true. God's promises become personal when we activate them by faith.

Do you want to experience more of God's promises in your life? Do you want to get the promises off the little card on the breakfast table and into your life? Then you must activate the promises by faith. Faith is what moves God's promises from your head to your heart!

If you've come this far in the book, then you already know three of God's great promises. Go ahead, review them. Our first promise is *God is always with me.* The second promise is *God is always in control.* The third is *God is always good.* Have they made any difference in your experience? It depends if you've activated them by faith. It's not enough to know something; you've got to put it into practice.

You can know all about a diet. You can list the rules and even write them out for someone else, but you're not going to lose weight unless you follow the plan yourself. You can be familiar with a piece of music, but it's not yours until you play it. A doctor's prescription of antibiotics can match your illness perfectly, but until you swallow it, it's not going to make any difference to your health.

You've got to take God's promises by faith. Only then will you see for yourself why they've satisfied generations of faithful men and women who've trusted God's Word.

Faith Is the Key

One time in the Gospels we are told that Jesus couldn't do much in a town **"because of their unbelief"** (Matthew 13:58). Wouldn't that be an awful thing to have said about your home, about your family, about *you*? Jesus couldn't do much in or through you because you didn't believe Him. *Lord, why don't You do more in our church?* Could it be because of people's unbelief? *Why do You make good things happen so often in my friend's life, but not in mine?* Could it be because your friend believes God more? Maybe you're a candidate for James's blunt wisdom—**"You do not have, because you do not ask. You ask and do not receive, because you ask wrongly"** (James 4:2b–3a).

Faith is the key. God's promises are activated by faith. Faith is not passive—it's an action. Don't say, *Well, I'm just waiting over here. Maybe God will work; maybe He won't.* What are you doing about it? Well, *not much,* you say.

At that point you are acting like the sick guy who needs to get better but won't go to the doctor. That's foolishness. You've got to do what you can.

Or like the young woman who is looking for a husband but never goes to the single adult meetings at church. She sits in her basement praying for her man to show up. *My husband will have to find me here.* Yeah, that's not a great plan—do your part!

Or the people who are filled with worry and want to have hope but have never read the Bible. They might carry it and respect it and defend it, but they're not living in it. They're not opening it like the Word of life and drinking from it like someone thirsting in a desert.

> *It isn't surprising that you don't have any hope! You're not holding on to anything that will sustain you.*

The next time you gather with other believers to cry out to God for rain, count how many people bring umbrellas for the trip home. Bringing an umbrella doesn't force God to send rain, but it does indicate how seriously we are expecting God to act!

God's promises give us hope. How many scriptural promises do you know by heart? Which ones are on the tip of your tongue?

Did you say, *Not a lot*?

Well, no wonder you're filled with anxiety! It isn't surprising that you don't have any hope! You're not holding on to anything that will sustain you.

Get your heart around some of the exceedingly great and precious promises of God! Hold on to what God has said in His Word. Someday you're going to be in a difficult situation and the enemy will try to pull you down, but he won't succeed, because you've got God's Word hidden in your heart. His words will flood you with courage and fill your life with faith.

Faith has to be active to be real. Remember Naaman in 2 Kings 5 who had leprosy, and God told him to go dip in the filthy Jordan River seven times? This guy didn't expect that healing would involve potentially humiliating circumstances. He would have paid for treatment but he wasn't all that eager to follow instructions. At first he was angry, but eventually, when he followed God's plan, he was healed. In faith, he did what he could. A

> *Only when we have done all we know to do can we wait by faith for God to do what only He can do.*

chapter earlier, remember the widow in debt who collected containers from her neighbors to hold all the oil God was giving her to pay back her creditor? In faith, she did what she could. A warrior heading into battle has to pick up his weapon, and we must do what we can, what we're commanded to do as an expression of faith.

Put some action behind what you believe and watch God work. Take a step and discover how God guides. Only when we have done all we know to do can we wait by faith for God to do what only He can do.

Making God's Promises Your Own

So, James, I know God is with me, *but now I want to* experience *His promises. How do I* know for myself that *God is in control? How do I personally* taste that God is good? Great questions!

Get God's promises happening at your house by taking these three practical action steps:

1. You've got to know if you have claim to certain promises. Examine God's Word very closely. Sometimes we don't see it for what it really is until we put it under a microscope. Have you ever read the Bible and all of a sudden a light bulb goes on over your head? The truth was there all the time but you just didn't see it. Part of this knowing involves understanding the promise in context. Some of the promises in God's Word are unique to particular situations and to certain people. For example, God made some promises to Samson that are not coming to you—no matter how you wear your hair. You could go to a lot of places in the Bible where God made specific promises to fit definite circumstances—and these promises are not personally relevant for you or for me. So you have to ask yourself, "Is this promise *unique* or is it *universal*?" Ask the Lord to show you, "Is this promise for me?"

One way you can know if a promise is universal is if God makes the same promise in other places in Scripture. For example, the idea that God is with His children is an irrefutable point. God promises multiple times that He will be with all of His children. Take a look for yourself: Genesis 26:3–5, Psalm 23:4; Isaiah 43:2; Matthew 28:20. Do you get it? Take hold of the promises that God has universally guaranteed to His children in all generations at all times. Ask God to open your eyes to the truth of it.

2. *You've got to savor the taste of God's promises.* If you want to experience God's promises for yourself, you've got to feed on them with your mind. Learn to treasure them in your heart. Allow them to nourish your soul. The law that the wise person in Psalm 1 meditates on day and night is flavored with God's promises. Tasting and seeing that the Lord is good has a lot to do with living with His promises.

Here's something that helps me, especially in my prayer life. You've got to picture the promise as already accomplished. It's been many years now, but our now college-aged son Landon almost died when he was born. I remember the evening we left the hospital and were told to say our good-byes as he likely would "not live through the night." As we sat and wept in our vehicle, praying in the dark parking garage, we pictured our prayers as answered. Having asked God to heal him, we added, *Lord we can see Landon grown and living for You—passionate and articulate as he shares Your Word. We can picture him by faith, blessing others and living for Your kingdom. Cause it to be so, we pray.* That was in 1988, before we even started Harvest. Now Landon serves effectively in our youth ministry, gives drum lessons to the mentally disabled, has graduated from Moody Bible Institute—God honored our faith for a fruitful life for our son and healed him. Practice picturing your prayers as answered and expressing that faith to God. Thank God in faith that it is already happening. *Even though it's not visual to me, God, by faith I believe Your Word. I believe that You are at work today bringing this about. You said You're with me, so I'm believing what You said and embracing the answer by faith.* Of course we pray according to God's will—and realize that God's picture may be different from what we ask. Be sure to end your prayers of faith with the important phrase, *Nevertheless, Lord, not my will but Yours be done* (see Matthew 26:39b). By adding that statement you are acknowledging that God's plan is always "more than all we ask or imagine"

(Ephesians 3:20 NIV).

3. You've got to share the results of God's promises. His promises will become real to you as you tell other people about them. *Here's God's promise that I'm resting in. I've already experienced His faithfulness in these ways.* Confess the Word of God with your mouth, following the pattern used in Romans 10:9 to establish salvation: **"If you confess with your mouth that Jesus is Lord and believe in your heart that God raised him from the dead, you will be saved."** There's power in speaking the Word out to express your inner faith. Say, "God's Word says *this.*" "I'm waiting on God for *that* result." "We're trusting God at our house for those benefits." When we give God credit in advance we're less likely to think of the outcomes as accidents or coincidences. Life will suddenly be full of God-incidents! When our church faced bankruptcy due to an incredibly difficult construction project, I used to walk through the partially completed building where no workers had been active for months and ask the Lord to overrule our errors in judgment. I would confess my own failures and ask God to intervene for the sake of His work and His name. I would confess out loud that the empty space I walked in was to be a house of salvation and a place where Jesus would be adored—"Right here!" I cried out, "Let Your name be exalted!" Today, those words are fulfilled multiple times each week and I believe God was merciful in answering those bold prayers confessing a reality that seemed impossible.

If you've embraced Jesus Christ as your Savior, then you've already activated by faith God's greatest promise. In Paul's greeting to Titus he says, **"Paul, a servant of God and an apostle of Jesus Christ, for the sake of the faith of God's elect and their knowledge of the truth, which accords with godliness, *in hope of eternal life, which God, who never lies, promised before the ages began...*"** (Titus 1:1–2, emphasis added).

Did you see the promise? **"In hope of eternal life."** A thousand years from today we'll all agree that this promise was the greatest one—the fact that in Christ we have the gift of eternal life. Today we believe that promise by faith until tomorrow when we will fully receive it. Notice another truth in verse 2: **"God, who never lies."** The New King James Version says, "God, who cannot lie." God is a promise keeper. So much of what we've been learning about the theology of a promise is right there in that phrase—we trust in the God who cannot lie.

*God looked through eternity past and He saw you and He
chose to reach out and redeem you by His own grace. It's hard to imagine
that kind of love. That's why He can't keep His eyes off of you!*

Radio teaching can sometimes feel like a one-way communication street. I can't look into the faces of people who are at the other end of the transmission waves. But the Internet often creates a two-way conversation. I read heartrending struggles out there.

> Dear Pastor James—
>
> I don't know if you read letters that are sent to you on your website. I hope so. I have to talk to somebody and what you said on your radio program today made me think that maybe you could help me.
>
> I could tell you about how bad my marriage is. I could tell you about my addiction to gaming. My son has this health problem that needs expensive medication and things don't look good at my job right now and if we lose the insurance, I don't know how we'll be able to take care of him. The men at my church try to help me but here's the problem—I don't think there's a way out of these problems. I was driving home on the freeway tonight and it was raining and I thought how easy it would be to drift into the other lane of

traffic and within seconds it would be over. I've never thought like that before and it scares me. People would never have to know how desperate I feel right now.

He signed the e-mail *Stephen*.

I dedicate this chapter to all the people, who, like Stephen, don't know if they're going to make it.

So far in our study of God's promises, we've talked about fearing and doubting, even having moments of despair. When you falter, you are overwhelmed by a severe problem that isn't going to get better in a couple days or even weeks. *Faltering* is a sober word that describes a person slipping down, going under, giving in, and losing the battle. The pressure to falter is great, and at times we would without an exceedingly great and precious promise. You need something larger and stronger than anything that might cause you to falter. Facing the overwhelming creates serious days. And serious days call for serious promises:

God is always watching: I will not falter.

I believe God promises that if you're walking in His strength by faith and embracing His promises, you're not going to falter. Isaiah 43:1 is one of the most treasured promises to God's children in all of God's Word. It begins, **"But now thus says the LORD, he who created you, O Jacob, he who formed you, O Israel: 'Fear not, for I have redeemed you; I have called you by name, you are mine.'"**

Now if we are going to make this promise our own, we have to understand the setting. The context in Isaiah 42 is that God's people are being judged. They were wayward and rebellious, and God was done with their attitude. The Lord was letting them feel the weight of all the garbage they had created by not trusting Him.

If you look at the whole chapter, you see their failure and the resulting fallout: **"Hear, you deaf, and look, you blind . . . [you] are . . . trapped in holes and hidden in prisons"** (vv. 18, 22). In verse 24, Isaiah asks, **"Who gave up Jacob to the looter, and Israel to the plunderers?"** And then he answers by way of another question, **"Was it not the LORD, against whom** we have sinned, in whose ways they would not walk, and whose law they would not obey?** Verse 25 continues, **"So he poured on him the heat of his anger and the might of battle; it set him on fire all around, but he did not understand; it burned him up, but he did not take it to heart."** God declared, through Isaiah, *I'm the one who piled all this on you and you're still not getting it.*

That is the background to the comfort that begins in the first verse of Isaiah 43: **"But now thus says the LORD, he who created you, O Jacob, he who formed you, O Israel: 'Fear not, for I have redeemed you; I have called you by name, you are mine.'"** Knowing the desperation of Israel's situation helps us recognize the priceless value of God's promise.

The Redeemer Who Goes with Us

Redemption is one of the greatest words in any language. We see its most glorious application on the cross of Jesus Christ. Before God interrupted your life, you were a slave to sin and had no way out. You owed a debt you could not pay—not even partially, or over time. You were bankrupt; morally, ethically, and spiritually broke. You were going to rot in debtor's prison, forever. But Christ showed up and redeemed you. He settled your debt. He paid the price so that you could be set free.

Don't be afraid, God says. *You have the worst possible problem, which requires the greatest imaginable sacrifice, and I took care of it.* It's kind of like this: You put your son all the way through college. You paid his tuition and helped him way more than he deserved. So today you're putting the final touches on his graduation party for tomorrow night and he shows up and says, "I'm not graduating."

"*What?!*"

"No, I owe twenty dollars on my book bill and they say I can't graduate."

So you open up your wallet and hand him the bill and say, "Son, after everything we've been through, don't you think we will take care of that too?"

That's what God says. *You think it's all over because you've got some problems? I redeemed you. What will I not do for you now? Fear not!*

Small problems seem big to us; but we're not God.

He's with us through the water

Ready for God's great and precious promise? Verse 2 says, **"When you pass through the waters, I will be with you."** "Waters" here is symbolic of a trial. If going through a valley isn't bad enough, now you're facing a flash flood. The water is rising rapidly. You cry out to God, "It's too deep! I'm going under!"

> *God leads us into difficult seasons, but He brings us through them. We emerge on the other side.*

What does God say in the first part of this exceedingly great and precious promise? **"When you pass through the waters, I will be with you."** *You're not going through this by yourself.* **"And through the rivers, they shall not overwhelm you."** *It might get deep, but it won't get too deep.* You might be thinking, "Help! It's over my head! We've been treading water at our house for over a year now." Well, who's holding you up? I know—it's the Lord! He is with you. The greatest treasure in this verse is the promise of His presence. At three places—*through* the waters... *through* the rivers... and *through* fire... He promises, *I will be with you.*

God leads us into difficult seasons, but He brings us through them. We emerge on the other side.

Too many times we're looking for ways to get *around* deep waters and dangerous fires, rather than *through* them. Has this ever been your experience? Have you tried to avoid a trial, only to have it move right in front of you again? That's God checking you, heading you off at the pass. He says you're going *through it because that's where you'll find Me.*

Pastoring one church for almost twenty-five years brings many forks in the road: a painful staff departure, a betrayal by a friend, deep disappointment as hypocrisy is uncovered and you wonder how many others are living a lie. Often in these seasons of adversity a letter or phone call will come offering a fresh start at a church in You-name-it. In that moment the temptation to "begin again" is very strong, but I believe persevering in one place with the same people has been the crucible of my sanctification. Going through the trial brings God's presence in a deeper way and is always better than finding a way to run.

You're going to get through this...

The word *through* is very closely related to the word *Hebrew*, the ethnic designation for the children of Israel. They are the ones who *go through*. By virtue of our spiritual heritage, we're those children, too; we're the children of God. We're the ones who *go through*. Some people go into stuff but they never come out. Not us! God leads us into difficult seasons, but He brings us through them. We emerge on the other side.

That's God's Word for someone reading this. *You're going to get through this. You're not going under; you're not going to be swept away.* **"When you walk through fire you shall not be burned."** Okay, it's going to get hot, but it's not going to get *too* hot. You're not going to get burned.

He's with us in the fire

Sometimes the Bible offers the best illustration of its own message. Do you remember Daniel's three friends, Shadrach, Meshach, and Abednego from Daniel 3? They stood for God in a very bleak time. They refused to bow and worship a golden image that a cranky, wicked King Nebuchadnezzar had set up of himself. They were respectful toward the king but unbending when it came to their ultimate allegiance to God. And the consequence they faced for their "disobedience"? Nebuchadnezzar was furious and commanded that the three men be brought before him. He told them, **"If you do not worship, you shall immediately be cast into a burning fiery furnace."** Then he asked, **"And who is the god who will deliver you out of my hands?"** (v.15). Great question! I guess Nebuchadnezzar hadn't gotten the memo.

"Shadrach, Meshach, and Abednego answered and said to the king, 'O Nebuchadnezzar, we have no need to answer you in this matter.'" Isn't that great?! What confidence! *We're not going to argue this point with you, sir. But we know who God is and it's not you.* **"'If this be so, our God whom we serve is able to deliver us from the burning fiery furnace, and he will deliver us out of your hand, O king. But if not, let it be known to you, O king, that we will not serve your gods or worship the golden image that you have set up'"** (vv.16–18). *Even if we don't get out of* *this alive, we'll still consider ourselves delivered, sir. With all due respect, your majesty, dead or living, we won't serve your gods or worship your statue.*

Clearly, Nebuchadnezzar was used to getting his way. The next two verses read, **"Then Nebuchadnezzar was filled with fury. . . . He ordered the furnace heated seven times more than it was usually heated. And he ordered some of the mighty men of his army to bind Shadrach, Meshach, and Abednego, and to cast them into the burning fiery furnace."** And they did. God could have stopped the murderers from going forward with the king's order, but He didn't.

Here's what happened next: **"Because the king's order was urgent and the furnace overheated, the flame of the fire killed those men who took up Shadrach, Meshach, and Abednego. And these three men, Shadrach, Meshach, and Abednego, fell bound into the burning fiery furnace.**

"Then King Nebuchadnezzar was astonished and rose up in haste. He declared to his counselors, 'Did we not cast three men bound into the fire? . . . But I see four men unbound, walking in the midst of the fire, and they are not hurt; and the appearance of the fourth is like a son of the gods'" (vv. 22–25). This is an *awesome* scene. Jesus Christ, preincarnate, second person of the Trinity was *with* them, just as He promised.

"Then Nebuchadnezzar came near to the door of the burning fiery furnace; he declared, 'Shadrach, Meshach, and Abednego, servants of the Most High God, come out, and come here!' Then Shadrach, Meshach, and Abednego came out from the fire. And the satraps, the prefects, the governors, and the king's counselors gathered together and saw that the fire had not had any power over the bodies of those men. The hair of their heads was not singed, their cloaks were not harmed, and no smell of fire had come upon them. Nebuchadnezzar answered and said, 'Blessed be the God of Shadrach, Meshach, and Abednego, who has sent his angel and delivered his servants, who trusted in him" (vv. 26–28). Because the three men had given credit to God ahead of time, the king had no doubts about who had delivered these men from his hand.

This true account from Daniel 3 helps me better understand Isaiah

43:2: **"When you walk through fire you shall not be burned, and the flame shall not consume you."**

He's Watching You Where You Are

Now if you're thinking to yourself, *Yes—that is an amazing story. But they're in the Bible and I live in Peoria!*

You've got to know that God sees you too. He's not missing a single detail in your life. He hears your conversations with your spouse. He sees your checkbook. He knows your unspoken fears. He's also watching the depth of the water. He's monitoring the heat of the fire. He's pouring out the strength that you need to endure in the minute you feel you can't go on. At this moment, God is watching your life and at some point in this trial, He will say *enough*. You don't need to falter.

This is why you need this fourth promise: *God is watching*. The problem is, if you have a wrong view of God's attention, you might not think this is so great. You may be wondering what exactly God is looking for as He monitors your life.

Wrong views of God's watching

Some people think that God watches them like a resentful relative. Kathy and I were recently at the wedding of a wonderful girl in our church. It was really something. The bride and her dad pulled up in a horse and buggy, both of their faces filled with joy. The ceremony was beautiful and we all gathered to send the bride and groom off to their honeymoon in Hawaii. As we applauded and laughed and bid them well, I was standing beside the bride's great-great-aunt. I heard her squawk to her husband, "I can't believe they're going to Hawaii. They're so young. They don't need to go to Hawaii. *I've* never been to Hawaii."

Some people think that God's like that. He's never excited about anything good that happens to you. But listen to these words of delight from Zephaniah 3:17: **"The LORD . . . will rejoice over you with gladness."** God is at the front of the balcony cheering on every good thing that happens in your life. Every wise decision you make, every blessing you receive and delight in, God is waving a flag and singing for joy. He is so *not* a resentful relative.

Some people think that God watches us like a hawk on the hunt. He's up there, circling at 10,000 feet, spying you out. He's just waiting for you to show some vulnerability and then—gotcha!—He will swoop down to grab you by the neck at your first wrong thought or action. Step out of line and you'll get snatched up. But God's not like that. Romans 8:1 makes this great promise: **"There is therefore now no condemnation for those who are in Christ Jesus."** Psalm 103:14 assures us that **"he knows our frame; he remembers that we are dust."** God knows the challenges that you face. He has given you in His Spirit and in

> These loving parents' eyes are glued to their precious child with that teary-eyed pride and joy. God loves you like that.

His Word everything you need for victory. You don't have to walk around on eggshells. God loves you. He wants to bless you and lavish loving-kindness upon you, filling your life with good things! Trusting in God's promises leads to bold living!

Some people think that God is watching us like the crabby Church Lady from old Saturday Night Live skits. In the church that I went to when I was growing up, there was a balcony that wrapped around the auditorium. Mrs. Martin always sat in the balcony and watched me. I know this because every time I would do something out of line, there she was, shaking her finger at me. *No, no, James.*

I felt bad writing that just now because the first time I ever preached in my church I was eighteen years old, and Mrs. Martin wrote me the nicest letter, thanking me and praying that God would use my life. As you get older, you see people differently, don't you? But maybe you're stuck in your focus on God as a crabby church leader. Maybe some difficult experience in your past has you convinced that God is never really quite happy with the choices that you're making. But God isn't like that either.

Psalm 31:8 says that "[**God has**] **set my feet in a broad place.**" You're not in danger of falling off the ledge with God. Make good choices, but make them to honor God, not because you wrongly view the Lord as some cranky, resentful person who does not delight in you.

Some people think that God is like a cantankerous boss. They imagine hearing God say, Do what I tell you and stop wasting my time. Get back to work! Stay late, work harder—it's never enough. That's not the way it goes with God at all. When He watches you, it is with the most loving, gracious, kind, benevolent interest in your well-being.

Occasionally at Harvest Bible Chapel we have a special Sunday when the kids' choir sings to the Lord. As they sing so beautifully, their parents fall all over each other to get their kid's picture. Every note and nuance is captured on video. As far as each mom or dad is concerned, their child is the only one in that chorus. They hear nothing but majestic music coming from their beloved. These loving parents' eyes are glued to their precious child with that teary-eyed pride and joy. *God loves you like that.* Don't let weird people from church, the controlling boss at work, or someone from your past cause you to misunderstand the wonderful truth that God is watching over you with perfect parental love. First John 4:16 says, "**So we have come to know and to believe the love that God has for us.**" Have you?

The Eyes of the Lord

Over and over, the Bible talks about the "eyes of the Lord" on us. *What does that mean?*

1. *The eyes of the Lord are inescapable.* Proverbs 5:21 tells us that "**a man's ways are before the eyes of the LORD, and he ponders all his paths.**" Proverbs 15:3 says, "**The eyes of the LORD are in every place, keeping watch on the evil and the good.**" God sees it all because He's watching.

2. *The eyes of the Lord are synonymous with what's right and true.* Deuteronomy 6:18 says, "**And you shall do what is right and good in the sight of the LORD, that it may go well with you.**" In the Old Testament, we read

about kings who **"did what was right in the eyes of the Lord,"** and leaders who **"did not do what was right in the eyes of the Lord."** *The eyes of the Lord* are constantly gazing on us and moving us toward what is good.

3. *The eyes of the Lord are focused upon and attentive to His own.* Imagine your neighborhood for a moment, let's say, from a Google Earth perspective. God is looking down at your block and knows the houses in which His children live. While God sees everything that happens on your street, He has a predisposition to fix His attention upon what's going on in the lives of His children and to extend a loving care toward us. His is not a zoomed- out glance from 30,000 feet; He's very focused on His own. First Peter 3:12 says, **"For the eyes of the Lord are on the righteous and his ears are open to their prayer. But the face of the Lord is against those who do evil."** Because you love Christ, God pays attention to you in a special and specific way.

4. *The eyes of the Lord are searching for people to bless.* God is looking for people on whom to show His favor. Second Chronicles 16:9 says, **"For the eyes of the Lord run to and fro throughout the whole earth, to give strong support to those whose heart is blameless toward him."** He's flat out looking for people who want to experience His strength. He's never tired of picking out His children in the crowd. He's looking for people on whose behalf He can show Himself strong.

5. *The eyes of the Lord are provoked to grace when He observes a righteous person.* Genesis 6:8 says that **"Noah found grace in the eyes of the Lord"** (nkjv). What a great challenge; what a great promise. I hope that when God sees you and me, He says, *Get more blessing over to that child; He loves My Son! And help her; she's following My way.*

Why does He watch?

Okay—I get it. God is watching me; His eyes are on me. The question now is, why? Why does God watch me? The answer is in Isaiah 43:3–4: **"For I am the Lord your God, the Holy One of Israel, your Savior. . . . Because you are precious in my eyes, and honored, and I love you."**

Do you remember in the introduction we talked about "precious" as a value word? Money is not precious—there's plenty of money around.

Education is not precious—educated fools are almost a proverb. But God's promises are precious and very great.

God tells you that **"you are precious in my eyes."** Hear me carefully on this: I'm not telling you that you are precious. You can find all kinds of pop-psychology preachers who'll tell you to simply believe you are precious. I don't think you are precious. I don't think I am either. I don't think that you or I have intrinsic value either. How many people are in the world—six billion? Out of all the world, I have some special value? No—I don't think so. What God says is better than *"You are valuable."* If God's heart for us hinges on value intrinsic to us, then what if we forfeit that value? No. God says something far better than that we are "valuable"—He declares us precious.

Precious means that we are valued—it is a choice God has made to set His love upon us. I have a clock in my home that is one of the most precious things I own. It once belonged to my grandparents who are the source of my life and faith. When I hear it chiming in the night, my heart is stirred with gratefulness to God for my rich heritage. You could easily and inexpensively purchase a higher quality clock—it keeps poor time and often breaks down. Yet it is exceedingly precious to me because of the value I place upon it. We are like that to God—not valuable but valued. And because our preciousness begins and ends with God, it can never change. You don't *have* value; *you're valued.* God has set a value upon you that is not intrinsic to you. Ephesians 1:4 says, **"he chose us in him before the foundation of the world."** Your value is based on what God has said about you. You didn't earn it or deserve it; you also can't lose it or forfeit it. *God* has determined your value. He has declared that you are precious in His sight.

Rather than saying, *I have value,* say this: *I am valued. I am precious to God in a way that is totally disproportionate to the person that I am.* That is an awesome truth. When God says that you are precious, that's a value word. That's also a time word—no one becomes precious in a moment.

Since the foundation of the world

This is a new thought for me: God has known me since the beginning of time. He chose to set His love upon me before He had even created the earth.

Psalm 139 tells me that before my days ever began, God knew them. God was intimately acquainted with me even as He was forming my body inside my mother's womb. The same is true for you.

No wonder Scripture says that you are precious to Him. He looked through eternity past and He *saw* you and He *chose* to reach out and redeem you by His own grace. It's hard to imagine that kind of love. That's why He can't keep His eyes off of you—because **"you are precious in [His] eyes, and honored, and [He] love[s] you"** (Isaiah 43:4).

No trial or temptation will take you down

Now for one of the greatest supporting promises in God's Word. These are the ones that spell out the details of the broad promises from our heavenly Father. First Corinthians 10:13 says, **"No temptation has overtaken you that is not common to man. God is faithful, and he will not let you be tempted beyond your ability, but with the temptation he will also provide the way of escape, that you may be able to endure it."** God is watching and He wants you to succeed at the Christian life. Considering His great love and honor toward you, do you honestly think He would let you go through more than you can handle? No. He won't let the waters drown you. He will keep the fires from burning you. He won't allow the temptation to be so strong it knocks you off your feet.

In Scripture's original New Testament language, there is just one word for "temptation" and "trial"; the same Greek word is used interchangeably, based on the intent of the passage. You can know if it means trial—an adversity allowed by God to transform me or a temptation—a solicitation to do evil that could never originate with God (James 1:13).

In 1 Corinthians 10:13, I believe both meanings are in view. God isn't going to allow either a temptation or a trial into your life that you won't be able to handle.

Again, temptation is a solicitation to do evil. It comes from Satan and is meant to pull you down. **"[God] himself tempts no one,"** we know from James 1:13. But a trial? That comes from God and is meant to change your character. Bottom line: Neither one is going to overtake your life.

The trial is not going to last forever and you will overcome it. God is faithful.

There is also no trial or temptation that you face that **"is not common to man."** Do you ever feel, *Nobody's going through what I'm going through?* That is simply not accurate. The enemy is trying to add "uniqueness" to your difficulties in order to make you falter. Don't fall for that! In the past, lots of people have gone through a trial like yours and even more are going through it in the future. You don't get singled out for a customized set of temptations. You're probably getting about average. No matter what's happening under your roof, you should be saying this: God is going to be faithful. Husbands, tell your wives. Wives, tell your husbands. Everyone tell your children and your neighbors: *We don't know what's going to happen today at home or at work or school but you need to believe God will be faithful. He will not allow us to be tried beyond our ability to withstand.* Let that promise comfort you.

> *The trial is not going to last forever and you will overcome it. God is faithful.*

I will not falter: God is watching. He's got His hand on the thermostat. The fire will not get too hot. He's watching the depth gauge; this trial will not get too deep. God actively controls the severity of everything we face.

Remember Job's story? Satan pressed his life with one trial after another, tempting him to curse God. The Lord allowed Satan to wreak havoc in Job's life, saying, **"Behold, all that he has is in your hand."** But God also put a limit to what Satan could do: **"Only against him do not stretch out your hand"** (Job 1:12). He does the same thing in our lives: *This far—no further, Satan,* God says. *That's all. That's my daughter. I know what she can handle. Not that much. Not there. Not now.* God protects His own. He will not allow you to be tested beyond what you are able to handle.

You might be thinking, *I'm already being tried beyond what I'm able!* The truth is, God knows you better than you know yourself. You're not going to lose it; you're going to be okay. You don't know what you are capable of when you're resting in God's strength and not your own. You're going to get through this one way or another. He is allowing you to go through a trial to change you and to bring glory to Himself. It's not going to last forever and you will get through it. God is faithful. He's not tired and He's not wondering when this is going to be over. The world's problems are not wearing Him out. He's God and He's watching.

Reassure yourself, *I'm not going to falter. I'm not going to lose it. I can keep going for another day, another week.* Lamentations 3:23 promises that God's mercies are new every morning. You just focus on getting through another day. As Jesus pointed out in Matthew 6:34, **"Sufficient for the day is its own trouble."**

Another Great and Precious Promise

When the time comes that you really can't take it anymore, 1 Corinthians 10:13 promises, **"He will also provide the way of escape."**

If you've been thinking, *I could really use an exit ramp right now, you will find one.* With practice you can learn to recognize "escapes" when you see them—they show up all the time. Here are some ways of escape God provides His children when they need them most:

- *God might end the trial right now.*
  He can pull you right out of the fire. *That's enough. You've learned it. I'm glorified in it. It's over.* Have you ever had that happen? I have. When God moves, the mountains get leveled; the floods get lowered; and the sun suddenly breaks through. Persevere and you will see God work on your behalf. In my experience, trials end as quickly as they start. Cancer treatment is a long process—three months of waiting for treatment followed by three months of radiation and then four more months of follow-up testing. Ten months is a long time to live with a cancer diagnosis. I found out in October, but then in a moment the following July I got the latest blood test results and I knew the cancer was behind me. So long in duration but then so quickly over. That can be the "way of escape."

- *He might give you encouragement to keep going.*

God will send some people along to encourage you so you know you're not alone. I remember a particular month of March that was my worst month ever. Day after day I felt I couldn't continue, yet God provided unsolicited support as my way of escape. Each week, out of the blue, four or five pastor friends of mine from other parts of the country called me on the phone. "James, you've been on my heart and I don't know why. I just want you to know that I love you and I'm praying for you." It happened every week and I can't explain it. Never before in my life have I experienced such spontaneous words of encouragement, and these calls and notes became God's way of escape for me. I realized, *I'm not alone in this trial.* It was God who prompted people's hearts to let me know they were praying, and His work in their lives became my escape from wanting to give up.

- *He gives you wisdom to act.*

Sometimes God gives wisdom and direction. Maybe you didn't know what to do, but God gave you wisdom. He showed you a new angle on the problem. And that one decision changed everything! I remember so many trials in ministry through the years that hinged for the good on a simple, God-given piece of wisdom.

- *He gives you strength to persevere.*

There are days when you don't think you will be able to get through it. You won't have the strength to face another morning at the office or another evening with that difficult person. *I thought I couldn't take it anymore; I can't believe how God has energized me for a new season of faithfulness. I know this didn't come from me.*

- *He gives you someone to share the burden.*

I felt so alone until God brought a friend back into my life. I turned a corner. We're walking this road together again and I think that I'll make it now. When we let others in on our struggles, God blesses our humility and dispels the darkness through the comforting assurance of friendship. That in itself is powerful comfort. Often God sends along a brother or sister who really *knows* and has gone through something similar. More than prayer for your strength, they bring an understanding of what's ahead. They stick closer than a sibling. The way of escape may be someone who has walked this road before.

• *He gives you a few days of relief.*

I just got away. God gave me an oasis in the middle of the desert. It replenished my reserves. Even Jesus sought moments of solitude and refreshment. Never underestimate the power of silence in God's presence as He draws near to you as no one else can. Maybe the circumstance will turn for a season, and though you had hoped it was over, looking back it was God giving you relief, a temporary way of escape so you could continue on.

Of course there are plenty more exit ramps than these, but suffice it to say, God will not allow you to be tempted beyond what you're able. He will make a way of escape. He doesn't promise you eight options, or six, or even three, but there will be at least one exit ramp. When you see it—turn off! Take the way out—whatever it is. It could be that a helicopter will fly over your situation and someone's arm will be reaching down to pick you up. Grab on to it! Sometimes God gets us out of situations in crazy, supernatural ways. Sometimes He gives us extra strength to remain in our trials, but one way or another, you will not falter because God is always watching. That is an exceedingly great and precious promise.

One closing thought. I want to write back to Stephen, the man who wrote me the e-mail I quoted at the beginning of this chapter. You can read over my shoulder if you want:

Dear brother Stephen,

Thanks for writing me. I often wonder where my words are going as they travel through the radio waves. You've helped me remember that real people are listening.

I can only imagine how dark the world feels right now to you. I've known a bit of that gloomy outlook myself in recent weeks. So I assure you with the strongest of confidence and conviction that God sees you in your situation. He's not going to let you drown. He loves you with an everlasting love. He won't let you get burned. He won't take His eyes off you. Even today He's shaping this trial into something that will make you into a strong man of God. You will be so glad when He reveals what He's up to.

Until that day, brother, keep your eyes on Him. Place your trust in Him. To do anything else will only make you falter and fail and fall on your face. Do whatever God asks. Look for His way of escape; not your own. And when you see His hand, take it—whatever that means. Humble yourself and He will lift you up. Rest completely in the promise that He is watching out for you. He's looking for people who want to experience His strength, on whose behalf He can show Himself strong. I think we both qualify!

Let's pray for each other until that day when we can say not only in faith, but also in testimony, that God has gotten us through.

Your brother in Christ,
James
2 Corinthians 4:7

Lord, I thank You today that You are so faithful. You are with me. You are in control. You are good. And You are watching. You know just when I'm in real need of a temporary or permanent way of escape—and You provide it! What an amazing truth that I can count on even though I may not see the exit until I need it. I don't have to fear no matter what circumstances come because You are with me. Thank You for the escapes You have already brought into my life. Cause me to remember them when I'm tempted to think that I'm stuck in a situation with no way out. With You, there's always a way out, through, around, or over! How good and faithful You really are. Amen.

TAKE TO HEART

GOD'S PROMISES ARE AN ASSURANCE GOD GIVES HIS PEOPLE SO THEY CAN WALK BY FAITH WHILE THEY WAIT FOR HIM TO WORK.

1. Can you remember a time when God provided an exit ramp or even a helicopter as an escape as we discussed back on page 122? How have you thanked Him? With whom have you shared that story of God's intervention?

2. How does the fact that God is watching over your journey today bring you comfort? Relief? Strength? Confidence? Think of an example in each category.

3. Difficult trials will naturally evoke powerful emotions in us. How would your circumstance look today if you chose to focus first on God's promises rather than how you feel? Reflect on this definition of faith: "Believing the Word of God and acting on it no matter how I feel because God promises a good result." How could you express faith today?

KNOW BY HEART
1 Corinthians 10:13

No temptation has overtaken you that is not common to man. God is faithful, and he will not let you be tempted beyond your ability, but with the temptation he will also provide the way of escape, that you may be able to endure it.

[THEOLOGY OF A PROMISE]

God is a Promiser by nature.

God keeps all of His promises.

God wants us to test His promises.

God's promises are activated by faith.

God's promises are experienced in Jesus Christ.

GOD'S PROMISES ARE EXPERIENCED IN JESUS CHRIST.

If I played the trumpet I'd be getting it out right now. I'd be taking deep breaths to give you a real blast of joy. Read 2 Corinthians 1:20 and see what I mean:

For all the promises of God find their *Yes* in [Jesus]. That is why it is through him that we utter our Amen to God for his glory.

All of God's promises are experienced in Jesus Christ. Doesn't that blow your mind?

Let's see how this applies to the ground we've already covered:

Promise 1: *God is always with me. I will not fear.* If you want to get more specific, it's Jesus Christ who's with you. Jesus says in Matthew 28:19–20, **"Go therefore and make disciples of all nations . . . teaching them to observe all that I have commanded you. And behold, *I am with you al-ways, to the end of the age*"** (emphasis added). Who's with me? It's Jesus Christ! He is the Promise of God.

Promise 2: *God is always in control. I will not doubt.* Hebrews 1:3 says that **"he upholds the universe by the word of his power."** It's Jesus Christ, the instrumentality of God the Father's sovereignty. Jesus Christ is the One who is holding the world He made in His hands.

Promise 3: *God is always good. I will not despair.* In John 10:11, Jesus said, **"I am the good shepherd."** He was telling us to count on Him to do all that a good shepherd does for his sheep.

Promise 4: *God is always watching. I will not falter.* Colossians 1:15–17 talks about Jesus' attentive interest in all that He has made. Jesus puts a personhood on the concept of God watching us. When we think about all the people Jesus met during His life here, it isn't hard to see that each person He spent time with felt exactly what he or she needed to feel under Christ's observation. His concentrated gaze conveys compassion. Relax under Jesus' watchful care.

And finally, Promise 5: *God is always victorious. I will not fail.*

Scripture tells us repeatedly that the One who is always victorious is Jesus Christ, the Mighty Warrior. Make no mistake about it; Jesus Christ is going to win. Someday the clouds will break open and we will see Him on a white horse (Revelation 19:11). Revelation 19:15 says that **"from his mouth comes a sharp sword with which to strike down the nations."** Furthermore, **"His eyes are like a flame of fire. . . . He is clothed in a robe dipped in blood, and the name by which he is called is The Word of God. . . . He will tread the winepress of the fury of the wrath of God the Almighty. On his robe and on his thigh he has a name written, King of kings and Lord of lords"** (vv. 12–13, 15–16). He will set the world in order in a big hurry with simply a *word!* Jesus Christ is going to win in the end.

All that to say God's promises are experienced in Jesus Christ. Romans 11:36 says of Him, **"For from him and through him and to him are all things."** Jesus Christ is the Promise of God!

Ephesians 2:14 says that Jesus Himself **"is our peace."** Do you need the calm assurance that God is in control? He doesn't dispense peace like a druggist fills a perscription: "Take this and call me in the morning." He promises us *Himself!* Jesus Christ *is* the Promises of God. He doesn't have to give you something; He *IS* the something.

It's Christ's presence that takes away fear.

It's Christ's sovereignty that gives us assurance and calmness in the face of doubts.

It's Christ's goodness that renews us when we are weighed down by despair.

It's Christ's watch-care and intervention that keeps us from faltering.

And it's Christ's inevitable victory that assures us we will not fail.

It's impossible to realize how important the promise of Jesus is unless you've experienced Him personally. I know for many years, to my shame, I flat-out didn't get this. I didn't even know I didn't get it. I grew up in a godly Christian home and went to a Bible-believing church, and I didn't get it. I went through Bible college and seminary and my first ten years in the ministry, and I still didn't get it.

In 1998, I was an inch away from leaving the ministry. For ten years I had put our church up on my shoulders every day, solving problems and dealing with people. I was exhausted and spent. The elders, sensing my desperate need, sent me away for a three-month sabbatical.

On a beach on the south coast of France, on my face before the Lord, I poured my tears into the sand and with finality admitted to God that "I can't do this anymore."

The Lord met with me in a way that forever altered my life. He spoke more clearly to me than He has at any other time. *James, admit it—you've hit the wall of impossibility when it comes to the Christian life. You're finally ready to let Me be that life in you. Get off the trying and failing merry-go-round! Let this be about Me from now on.*

My reading companion during those weeks was a powerful book called *The Saving Life of Christ*. It was written the year I was born, 1960, by Major W. Ian Thomas, an evangelist and founder of the Torchbearer Bible School and Conference Center. Many of the truths that are central in my current ministry were first planted in my heart and mind by that book and other books it has led me to. Most important, that book gave me a fresh look at God's Book.

On July 12, 1998, while in England and reflecting on Thomas's insights, I wrote this prayer on the bottom of a page: "Lord, I am so weak! Every day of failed effort to live a righteous life is painful and a penetrating truth of that fact. But today I turn as never before to You alone. Christ, live in me. I die to myself by faith, and today, Lord, I trust You to live Your life through me."

Simple words, but a powerful turning point in my life. I commend it to you this moment—the exchanged life. That simple truth has absolutely changed my life, and it can change yours too. This brief life-changing experience and the truth that Christ is the power to live the Christian life, "not I, but Christ in me" (see Galatians 2:20)—was recorded in my first book on change more than ten years ago.[3] After a decade of living these truths I cannot imagine going through a valley without them.

Of course this is all laid out for us in Scripture. We all know Romans 5:8: **"But God shows his love for us in that while we were still sinners, Christ died for us."** Verse 10 continues, **"For if while we were enemies we were reconciled to God by the death of his Son, much more, now that we are reconciled, shall we be saved by his life."** It's the *life* of Jesus Christ. Do you *get* it? He died for our sins but then He rose from the dead to live His life through us.

Here it is in a sentence that encapsulates it for me: God has made no provision for you to live the Christian life on your own. The Christian life is ***Christ in you, the hope of glory*** (Colossians 1:27).

This truth changed my life. Jesus Christ *is* the Christian life. It's not me acting like Jesus. That's just religion: performing and "look at me" and trying to be a Christian—which gets stale, ritualistic, and exhausting pretty quickly. Then it isn't long before we throw everything up in the air and say, "I can't *do* all this!"

Correct, He never said we could. Instead, the Christian life is all about yielding to the living presence of Christ *in* me by His Spirit. He *is* the Christian life.

I remember preaching on 2 Corinthians 4:8–9: **"We are afflicted in every way, but not crushed; perplexed, but not driven to despair; persecuted, but not forsaken; struck down, but not destroyed."** Isn't that great news? But I shouldn't have stopped there! The next verse explains how all those things happen. How is it that I am afflicted, but not crushed; perplexed, but not in despair; persecuted, but not forsaken; struck down, but not destroyed? How? Crazy—I didn't even see it!

Second Corinthians 4:10, the next verse, answers how those wonderful promises come true. Here's how: **"Always carrying in the body the death of Jesus, so that the life of Jesus may also be manifested in our bodies."**

Again, **"I have been crucified with Christ,"** teaches Galatians 2:20. **"It**

is no longer I who live, but Christ who lives in me." Jesus *is* the Christian life. Do you get it? It's not you trying to please the Lord, or to thank Him, or impress Him, or even trying to imitate Him. The core of this truth is: *It's Christ in me by His Spirit.*

Why do you think Jesus told the disciples in Acts 1:4–8 to get in a room and wait for the Holy Spirit and not to do *anything* else? Because without His Spirit they were worthless and so are we.

Look at the disciples in the Gospels. They were wavering, wallowing, weak followers of Christ. But when the Spirit of God came upon them they **"turned the world upside down,"** says Acts 17:6. The Spirit of Jesus Christ is your power! First Thessalonians 5:16–24 has meant so much to me in this regard.

---

1 THESSALONIANS 5:16–24

Rejoice always, pray without ceasing, give thanks in all circumstances; for this is the will of God in Christ Jesus for you. Do not quench the Spirit. Do not despise prophecies, but test everything; hold fast what is good. Abstain from every form of evil.

Now may the God of peace himself sanctify you completely, and may your whole spirit and soul and body be kept blameless at the coming of our Lord Jesus Christ. He who calls you is faithful; he will surely do it.

At first blush this passage looks like a grocery list of all the "stuff" we have to do in the Christian life. 1. Rejoice always. 2. Pray without ceasing. 3. Give thanks in all circumstances, and more. Like a juggler trying to keep all the balls in the air, maybe we just need to get more skillful in the Christian life, add more disciplines, get more dedicated, increase our capacities for even more, and on and on.

But that's not it at all.

If we go directly to 1 Thessalonians 5:24 it says, **"He who calls you is faithful; he will surely do it."** He doesn't just *call* me to it, He *does* it. Once again, Jesus Christ *is* the Christian life.

I realized that day on the beach before the Lord that I hadn't understood this before. If I could in any way help you take a shortcut and learn this from me now, it would spare you so much frustration! Have the crisis now and save yourself years of struggle. It's Christ *in* you that lives the Christian life.

Some of you are like, "Too late. I've lived many years of failure and frustration not understanding that I didn't have to do it, but that Christ does it in me." All the more reason to have the crisis at this moment. In fact, that's really the question: *Have you had that crisis in your life where you recognize that your ability to sanctify yourself is similar to your ability to save yourself?* Could you save yourself? No, you could not. Can you sanctify yourself? Right—same answer.

Colossians 2:6 says, **"As you received Christ Jesus the Lord, so walk in him."** The same total dependence you expressed when you surrendered to the Lord—*Please save me, Lord, I can't do this myself*—is the same, total broken spirit that you need to approach living the Christian life. *I can't do this on my own. I can't make myself read the Bible. I can't make myself hate sin. I can't make myself godly.* A growing, personal, dynamic intimacy with Jesus is the only hope for the Christian life. You can't comfort yourself. You can't convince yourself about these promises. You've got to connect with Jesus and let *Him* make these things real to you. It's all about that.

God's Promises Are Experienced in Jesus Christ

Again, if I played the trumpet, I'd be making some noise right now. We're on the bull's-eye of this whole book. You want to experience the exceeding great and precious promises of God? Find yourself in Jesus Christ. Remember the verse at the beginning of this chapter? **"For all the promises of God find their Yes in him. That is why it is through him that we utter our Amen to God for his glory"** (1 Corinthians 1:20).

Look closely at this phenomenal verse. Read it over again: **"For all the promises of God find their Yes in him. That is why it is through him that we utter our Amen to God for his glory."** Is there anything more thrilling than to point to Christ and say, *Look at Him! He's everything! All*

God's promises find their "Yes" in Him! Yes and Amen!

If it wasn't for Jesus Christ, who could stand?

If it wasn't for Jesus Christ, could any of us be faithful?

If it wasn't for Jesus Christ, who could endure a trial?

Come to the end of your self-oriented efforts and lay your life down. Nothing of me; all of Him. *Amen?*

God's promises are experienced in Jesus Christ. If you are peaceful, resting, and trusting in His Word, that's a good sign that you're getting it! If you're striving, worrying, and feeling spent, that's a clear sign that you're calling the shots and carrying the weight and figuring it all out on your own. It's one way or the other—which is it going to be?

Jesus Christ the Lord, who is Himself all the Promises of God, will be forever victorious. I've read to the end of the Book, and God wins.

Promise #5: **GOD IS ALWAYS VICTORIOUS**

(I will not fail)

"No weapon formed against you shall prosper, and every tongue which rises against you in judgment you shall condemn. This is the heritage of the servants of the LORD, and their righteousness is from Me," says the LORD. Isaiah 54:17 (NKJV)

I've spent a lot of time lately thinking about trials. At the end of day, if you pinpoint what's difficult about the trial, it's the *not knowing*. The biggest reason why I fear and doubt, despair and falter—is that I don't know how it's all going to end.

Stay with me on this. Think of the situation that caused you to read this book, that keeps you awake at night—that issue that lingers on the edges of your thoughts and never fully goes away. If you knew definitively right now how that circumstance was going to end, you would be okay. Am I right? If you could foresee it ended well, you could bear the waiting. If you saw it ended badly, you could prepare yourself for what's to come. It's the *not knowing* that pushes us to the limit.

A football team doesn't get all sideways because they lose a few yards. As long as they win the game, it's all good. *How does my trial finish? What's the final score?* That's what I need to know. And that is where our fifth and final exceedingly great and precious promise comes in.

You're Not Alone

Before we dive in, let's acknowledge that every one of us lives with some level of uncertainty. I don't want you to feel like you're alone in this struggle. You've got some insecurity in your life right now; I'm living with some question marks too.

How Jeff makes it

We've got this great guy on our staff named Jeff Donaldson. He's one of our church's most treasured and gifted leaders. Not only is he a fruitful and effective communicator, but he's also a great dad to his five kids and is very committed to the cause of Christ.

Six years ago Jeff was diagnosed with a pituitary brain tumor and it absolutely changed him. Before his health crisis, he certainly had been successful, but since his recovery, I tell you, Jeff is a powerful force for God.

A couple weeks ago we had a "Young Preacher Weekend" in our services and Jeff preached his heart out. What nobody knew was that he was hurting pretty badly. We had just come home from a staff retreat at our church camp, where we had played a game that our mothers certainly would have said was "fun until someone gets hurt." And that's exactly what happened. One of our larger pastors used his significant size to take Jeff out. Our big guy (whom we love too) powered down right on top of Jeff, knocking the wind out of him and breaking a couple of his ribs.

When Jeff got home he went to the hospital for X-rays. Then the doctor wanted to do an MRI. Then some more tests. Jeff went into the hospital looking for some help with his broken ribs but got the news that there were some unexplainable spots on his lungs. Jeff told a couple of people so they could pray, but then just waited for the results.

Meanwhile, the whole time he's preaching his guts out; inside he's living with uncertainty. *What's going to happen? Is this cancer? If it is, then what? What about my wife and my kids?* He had more tests the following Monday and even more on Tuesday. On Thursday he sent me an e-mail: *It's totally fine.* The spots were bruises from the broken ribs.

If you've ever been sick, really sick, then you know that every trip to the hospital is stressful. Every test drains you. *Is the cancer back? Will I be okay this time?*

Jeff's health will always be an uncertainty for him. He will never routinely visit the doctor like other people do. He has to live with the possibility that his health crisis could return. Every day he has to hold on to God's promises and walk by faith. But that's exactly what we all should be doing. We all have areas of uncertainty. You may relate directly to a health crisis, or your questions about the unknown may concern a family member. Perhaps you are facing a business crisis. *I just don't know where all of this is going to end up . . .*

That's why I'm so thankful for Promise #5: *God is always victorious; I will not fail.*

I know how this all ends—God wins. Isaiah 54:17 says, "**'No weapon formed against you shall prosper, and every tongue which rises against you in judgment you shall condemn. This is the heritage of the servants of the LORD. And their righteousness is from Me,' says the LORD**" (NKJV).

This is one of my absolute favorite verses in the whole Bible. God made this awesome assertion to the postexilic Israelites as they came back to the land that He had promised them. Judgment was over and now blessing was coming. God gave them this promise and extended it by His grace to all of His children.

No weapon will succeed against you

"**No weapon formed against you shall prosper.**" In the Hebrew language, "weapon" means "any tool or utensil used against a person." A weapon is *anything* anyone would use against you for evil intent.

If anyone would use their *car* against you, it "**shall not prosper.**"

If anyone would use their *cell phone* against you, it "**shall not prosper.**"

If anyone would use their *checkbook* against you, it "**shall not prosper.**"

Nothing "**formed against you shall prosper.**" Nothing built, sharpened, aimed, or fired against you, your family, your church family, God's kingdom, or God's people will succeed. They may seem to win for a while—a job may be lost; a child may wander and be lost; and a life may even be lost—but in the end even these tragedies will assist God's prospering of those who are truly His.

The Lord fights for you

I like the confidence in Joshua 23:10: **"One man of you puts to flight a thousand. . . ."** *How could I ever chase away a thousand people?* Here's how: **". . . since it is the LORD your God who fights for you, just as he promised you."** The reason **"no weapon formed against you shall prosper"** is not because you are some impressive warrior now that you're working out. It's because **"it is the LORD your God who fights for you."** He is the Defender of His children.

> Do you know what it's like to be scorned because of your stand for God's truth? Have you been rebuked because of your fidelity to God's agenda? If you have to answer no to these questions, it's not a good sign.

The promises God gave to His people back then remain eerily applicable today. I'm sure you have heard threats from Iran's president, Mahmoud Ahmadinejad. He has said, among other things, that Israel "has reached the end of its function and will soon disappear off the geographical domain."[4] Is that what he thinks? Well, I'm going to put my money with God on that one. God has made some promises about His protection to a literal Israel and He's going to keep them. If you want to encourage your heart, study the incredible journey of the Jewish people. In spite of what God has allowed them to go through and the blindness that veils their eyes during this current season when the church is being grafted in (Romans 11), study how God has protected and preserved Israel as a people. *I don't know what's going to happen exactly, but here's what God promises:* **"No weapon formed against you shall prosper."**

The word "prosper" gives us hope. The English Standard Version uses the word "succeed." The New International Version says, "prevail." Here's the point: No weapon will be final. Even if it looks like it's prospering; it's not done yet. It may win the battle, but it won't win the war. God takes it very seriously when someone opposes or attacks the ones He loves.

But James, you may say, *it's not their weapons that bother me. It's their words.*

And I can assure you, *Their words will not win either.* Look at the next phrase in Isaiah 54:17: **"Every tongue which rises against you in judgment you shall condemn."** Have you ever been a target for hurtful words because of your stand for the Lord? Have you experienced ridicule where you work or where you live because of your loyalty to Christ? Do you know what it's like to be scorned because of your stand for God's truth? Have you been rebuked because of your fidelity to God's agenda? If you have to answer *no* to these questions, it's not a good sign. It most likely means that the people around you haven't noticed any direct connection between you and God. More of us need to ponder what Paul pointed out to Timothy: **"Indeed, all who desire to live a godly life in Christ Jesus will be persecuted"** (2 Timothy 3:12). If we never risk standing for Christ; we never discover the faithfulness of God's promises.

God promises in Isaiah 54:17 that those who rise against you won't have the last word. Second Thessalonians 1:6 affirms that God will have the final say: **"Since indeed God considers it just to repay with affliction those who afflict you."** Is someone making it hard for you? Resisting you? Challenging you? Someday God will call you forward and you'll see those who rose against you. God will say, *Do you remember all the stuff they said was going to happen and how it was going to end up? Well, that's all over now.* And you will actually be able to say, "You said I was wrong but God's Word has proven itself true. *I wasn't* foolish to trust the Lord Jesus Christ." The slanderers shall be silenced, proven conclusively to be in error and justly condemned. If you've experienced pain from others who oppose you and God's will for your life, and who oppose God's blessing on your family, Isaiah 54:17 is for you.

God is keeping a record of everyone who doesn't get under His grace and mercy. Don't wish this upon anyone. Someday those who reject God's mercy will hear the condemning news of almighty God, and it will be voiced by you: **"You shall condemn,"** to which you probably will object, *But I fail the Lord in so many ways. I don't really think I deserve to . . .* Correct, you don't. That's why the verse says, **"'This is the heritage of the servants of the Lord, and *their righteousness is from Me,'* says the Lord"** (emphasis added). Our righteousness is not our own, it is from the Lord. It's for God's own glory that this is going to happen. It's not because you are something extra special. It's because you're one of God's children and He has set His love upon you. Even if *you* don't understand in fullness what this all means, let me tell you: God gets it. He's got it covered. He knows what it means that you're one of His.

> Someday soon we're all going to be in eternity and we'll be amazed at how life raced by.

The enemy comes along and accuses, "How do you deserve that kind of a position?" You say, "I don't. My righteousness is from Christ. I *don't* deserve to have this favor with God. I *don't* deserve the protection of God, but my righteousness is from Him." That's the power and the glory of the gospel. **"It is no longer I who live, but Christ who lives in me"** (Galatians 2:20).

God is always victorious

God always wins! Romans 16:20 gives us the fantastic news that it's going to end like this: **"The God of peace will soon crush Satan under your feet."**

Let's talk about the "when this is going to happen" part first. The Bible says "soon." I think that means *sooner than you think.* Someday soon we're all going to be in eternity and we'll be amazed at how life raced by. On that day, I'm going to find you and be like, *I told you this was coming fast!* Eternity is racing upon us. This story will soon be in its last, and glorious, chapter. So, anytime it feels like a day is dragging by, get in the habit of praying, *Soon, Lord. Soon.*

Next, let's talk about the "crush Satan under your feet" part. What kind of shape will Satan be in after this happens? Not great. He'll be *crushed.*

Here's a shocker—God will crush Satan under *your* feet. Think of every battle and struggle you have endured that was prompted by the enemy of your soul. Every temptation that clawed at you, every painful attack on your body and in spirit, all brought on by Satan—and your foot will rise up and *crush him*. God will make it so.

> *Today is your opportunity to prove the superiority of the life lived in Jesus Christ. Now is the time not to be held back!*

The first promise in the Bible, found in Genesis 3:15, foretells that Jesus will have the final victory and will **"crush [his] head"** (NIV). Satan will be rendered inoperative and then cast with all of his demonic hosts into the lake of fire. This is the **"second death,"** Revelation 20:14 says.

Today is my chance to honor God

I ran some track in high school. There were days when the race seemed so long that I didn't think I could run one more step. But then within an hour, I'd look back and think, *I could have done a little more. I could have gone a little longer.* We all know that feeling. We're in the ultimate race now; it's called life. Before we know it, it's going to be over. I don't want to look back and say, *I could have gone further in my walk with God. What held me back?*

Today is your chance to honor God. This is your opportunity to prove the superiority of the life lived in Jesus Christ. Now is the time not to be held back!

Just like you, I have uncertainties. I have health concerns. I have burdens in my family and in my marriage and in my career. I'm going through the same struggles that the people who don't know Christ are going through. The difference is, I have the Lord. I have the Spirit of God alive inside me. I have the grace to love when I'm hated. I have the strength to give when I'm taken advantage of. I have a supernatural capacity as one of God's sons or daughters to live in Christ.

I have the promises of God.

I'm running today with my eyes on that final day. **"Then I saw a great**

white throne and him who was seated on it. From his presence earth and sky fled away, and no place was found for them" (Revelation 20:11). Jesus Christ the Lord, who is Himself all the Promises of God, will be forever victorious. The end! I've read to the end of the Book, and God wins.

I will not fail: God is always victorious. His purposes are always accomplished. His enemies are always defeated. His faithful followers are always rewarded. His Son's throne will be established forever.

God's promises are always true.

Lord, Jesus Christ, come and live Your life through me. Let my life be a demonstration of the living presence of Christ. Forgive me for trying to live my life in my own strength. Help me as I embrace these promises by faith. Thank You, God, that You are with me in this as I seek to live for You and to honor You and to bring You glory. Thank You that You are always with me.

TAKE TO HEART

GOD'S PROMISES ARE AN ASSURANCE GOD GIVES HIS PEOPLE SO
THEY CAN WALK BY FAITH WHILE THEY WAIT FOR HIM TO WORK.

Encourage someone today who is going through a trial caused by someone else's sin with the news that you know how their story ends—God wins!

Next, remind yourself of the five exceedingly great and precious promises that we've studied here. Which one(s) do you need to put your whole weight down on today as you're waiting for God to work?

Promise #1: ***God Is Always with Me.***
I Will Not Fear.
Promise #2: ***God Is Always in Control.***
I Will Not Doubt.
Promise #3: ***God Is Always Good.***
I Will Not Despair.
Promise #4: ***God Is Always Watching.***
I Will Not Falter.
Promise #5: ***God Is Always Victorious.***
I Will Not Fail.

Which of the "theology of a promise" truths do you need to engage?

God is a Promiser by nature.

God keeps His promises.

God wants us to test His promises.

God's promises are activated by faith.

God's promises are experienced in Jesus Christ.

KNOW BY HEART
Isaiah 54:17

"No weapon formed against you shall prosper, and every tongue which rises against you in judgment you shall condemn. This is the heritage of the servants of the LORD, and their righteousness is from Me," says the LORD. (NKJV)

A Final Note of Encouragement

This book has come to an end—but not the promises of God. Each of the ones we've explored here can be proven true throughout your life! Not to mention that we've chosen only five of the many promises of God waiting for you in His Word. Get in the habit of highlighting God's promises every time you find them in Scripture. I've known people who write in the margins of their Bibles, next to God's underlined promises, significant dates when they have seen that particular promise again proven true for them. Think of the ways God has demonstrated His faithfulness to you and let others know—not to make yourself look good but to encourage them to see God's faithfulness in their own lives.

Go ahead, take me up on this! If you will make it a point to note specific examples of God's promises fulfilled in your life, you will experience the rolling snowball effect—a gradual building of an avalanche of God's blessings in your life. I'm amazed when I give groups of believers "the floor" in order to shout out their personal examples of God's faithfulness and then watch brows furrow as if God's promises were a rarely seen phenomenon! If we have to think hard to come up with God's blessings, we must be walking around with our eyes firmly shut, our ears closed, and our hearts hard.

Because God keeps His promises every single day, the opportunity to share what we are experiencing ought to have the effect of floodgates opening at the foot of a dam—a powerful explosion of praise and honor to God for His faithfulness. Too many of us live below the dam, looking up at the towering, dry walls, half-believing the whispers that there's nothing up behind the dam—the walls are holding back nothing! Decide you're going to live your life on top of the reservoir, watching God's promises create such an overflow that you simply have to open the floodgates and relieve the pressure! David's best known psalm has a line in it that unfortunately gets overlooked—**"My cup overflows"** (Psalm 23:5c). That line comes after a sequence of four huge fulfilled promises. Here they are: **"You are with me"** (v. 4b); **"Your rod and your staff they comfort me"** (v. 4c); **"You prepare a table"** (v. 5a); **"You anoint my head with oil"** (v. 5b)—no wonder David's cup is overflowing!

You can live that overflowing life. Make it your daily practice to track the carry-over of God's faithfulness from yesterday and the accumulation of His blessings today, and then let the results spill over into other lives. It's never a question of competition over whose cup is most full—encourage others to enjoy the overflow of God's promises by helping them spot what God has been doing in them and for them. You can have a powerful ministry of one-on-one conversations in which you begin, "I could hardly wait to tell you the ways I've noticed God's promises working in your life!" They will be all ears!

Acknowledgments

I am thankful for almost everyone; every person who stood with us during the darkest season of our lives. It was not easy to keep our hand on the plow when it seemed we had lost our way in the field. I am very thankful for those who stood with us and encouraged us all the way through.

Rick Donald, our assistant senior pastor since the beginning of time (it seems) and his wife, Lyn. Kathy Elliott, my personal assistant over that same period. Luke Ahrens, also assisting in my office and now a Harvest Bible Chapel church planter in Columbus, Ohio. I am thankful for Robert and Mary Jones, Fred Adams our CFO, Bill Molinari, and Kent and Nancy Shaw.

I am truly thankful for the incredible poise and commitment displayed by Janine Nelson, the executive director of Walk in the Word. I am thankful for these and many others; the Ministry Leadership Team and staff of Harvest Bible Chapel. Scott Pierre, the chairman of Walk in the Word, his family, and the other board members who have continued with us in faith.

I am thankful for every servant of Christ who remains with us to these sunny days—seeing fruit and blessing and joy in ministry more than ever before. I am thankful for our church family that has been in the crucible of my sanctification and the playing field upon which I tested God's promises. The constancy of their love and prayers I am sure is what made all the difference. I am thankful for gifted writing partners at Moody and for Neil Wilson, as well. Robert Wolgemuth and the team at Wolgemuth and Associates are also to be sincerely thanked.

The list could become very long. There are many wonderful new people on our ministry team today, but always the ones who endured the storm are most precious to any survivor. Most of all, together and on our knees with hands raised to the sky, we thank the Lord, the God of promise who has made good on everything He said. EVERYTHING! ☺

James MacDonald
Fall, 2010

Scripture Index

Acts 17:29
Acts 17:30
Romans 12:16–20
1 Corinthians 2:9
1 Corinthians 13:4–7
Galatians 3:29
Ephesians 1:11
Ephesians 3:20
Ephesians 4:2–3
Ephesians 4:15–16
Ephesians 4:29–32
Hebrews 6:11–12
Hebrews 6:13–15
Hebrews 6:17–19
Hebrews 11:8–19
Hebrews 13:8
James 1:6

Promise #3

Exodus 14:13–14
Deuteronomy 6:16
Deuteronomy 11:26–28
Joshua 21:45
1 Kings 8:56
1 Samuel 13:14
Psalm 27:13
Psalm 33:11
Psalm 34:8
Psalm 46:10
Psalm 100:5
Psalm 119:140
Psalm 145:9
Isaiah 30:15
Isaiah 40:8
Jeremiah 29:11
Lamentations 3:25
Nahum 1:7
Matthew 4:7
Matthew 6:33
Romans 8:28
Philippians 4:19

Promise #4

Genesis 6:8
Genesis 26:3–5
Deuteronomy 6:18
2 Chronicles 16:9
Job 1:12
Psalm 23:4
Psalm 31:8
Psalm 103:14
Proverbs 5:21
Proverbs 15:3
Isaiah 42:18
Isaiah 42:22
Isaiah 42:24
Isaiah 42:25
Isaiah 43:1–4
Lamentations 3:23
Daniel 3:15–18
Daniel 3:22–25
Daniel 3:26–28
Zephaniah 3:17
Matthew 6:34
Matthew 13:58
Matthew 26:39
Matthew 28:20
Romans 8:1
Romans 10:9
1 Corinthians 10:13
2 Corinthians 4:7
Ephesians 1:4
Ephesians 3:20
Titus 1:1–2
James 1:13
James 4:2–3
1 Peter 3:12
2 Peter 1:4
1 John 4:16

Promise #5

Genesis 3:15
Joshua 23:10

Psalm 23:4–5
Isaiah 54:17
Matthew 28:19–20
John 10:11
Acts 1:4–8
Acts 17:6
Romans 5:8
Romans 5:10
Romans 11:36
Romans 16:20
1 Corinthians 1:20
2 Corinthians 1:20
2 Corinthians 4:8–9
2 Corinthians 4:10
Galatians 2:20
Ephesians 2:14
Colossians 1:15–17
Colossians 1:27
Colossians 2:6
1 Thessalonians 5:16–24
2 Thessalonians 1:6
2 Timothy 3:12
Hebrews 1:3
Revelation 19:11
Revelation 19:15
Revelation 20:14
Revelation 20:11

Notes

1. August 4, 2005 *CNN Larry King Live* transcript.

2. http://www.alsirat.com/lastwords/utoz/jwesley.html.

3. For more on this topic, see James MacDonald, *I Really Want to Change...
So Help Me, God!* (Chicago: Moody, 2000).

4. http://jeffreygoldberg.theatlantic.com/archives/2008/06/mearsheimer
_and_walt_apologist.php.

WHEN LIFE IS HARD

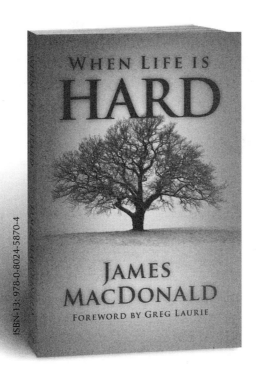

When life is hard, you know, really hard, we often spend all our time pleading, begging, yelling, refusing, and questioning. While none of these things are necessarily unusual, they are missing the ultimate point. When life is hard, when things get ugly, when all hope seems to be lost, that is when we are able to display the superiority of the life lived in God. It is in those moments of despair, when we question what is happening, when we don't know what to do, when some trials never seem to end, that we can lean most heavily into God's promises and truths.

MOODY
PUBLISHERS

moodypublishers.com

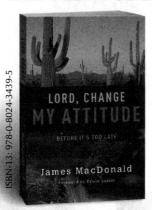
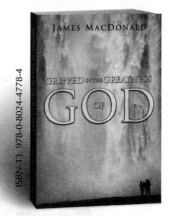
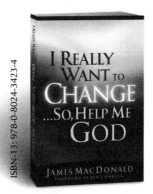
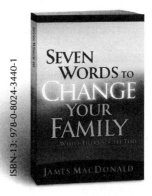

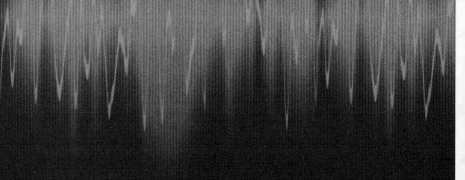